W9-ARG-574

# WHAT IS PHILOSOPHY?

# WHAT IS PHILOSOPHY?

## *A Short Introduction*

ELMER SPRAGUE

BROOKLYN COLLEGE

NEW YORK OXFORD UNIVERSITY PRESS

To
My Brooklyn College Students
"NIL SINE MAGNO LABORE"

# Preface

The advent of the paper-backed book has worked a revolution in the teaching of philosophy. With everyone able to afford his own collection of basic writings, students are now reading the great philosophers for themselves; and in philosophy classes, formal lectures are giving way to class discussions of original texts. Because philosophy is to most students the one entirely new subject which they meet in college, they may find a preliminary survey of the subject useful. This book's aim is to acquaint the beginning philosophy student with the plan of the forest before he is hopelessly lost among the trees. The topics covered—human knowledge, the world, God, human freedom, morals, and politics —are most often regarded as the core of philosophical studies.

This book had its origin in Brooklyn College's required philosophy course, Knowledge and Values. All kinds and conditions of students read and discuss large chunks of original works on a wide range of topics; and the instructor who would make the conclusions of philosophy clear to all of them must develop skills and stamina resembling those of a catch as catch can wrestler. My own teaching owes much to my teachers at the University of Nebraska and at Oxford. In addition I have profited greatly from many conversations with my colleagues Professor Martin E. Lean and Professor Paul W. Taylor. Finally, I wish to record my thanks to my wife, Gretchen, who encouraged me as I wrote and who cheerfully typed and retyped my several visions and revisions.

E. S.

*Brooklyn, N. Y.*
*Lammastide,* 1960.

# A Note on Collateral Reading

At the head of each chapter there are suggested for joint reading those books and other items which either are discussed in the chapter or are immediately relevant to the topics covered in the chapter. At the end of each chapter there is a brief list of books and essays which are especially recommended as the next step in reading on the topics covered in that chapter. When a book is available in several different paperback editions, title and author are cited. When a book is available in only one paperback edition, title, author, and publisher are cited. When a book is available only in a hard-cover edition, title, author, publisher, and place and date of publication are cited. I cannot emphasize too strongly that my suggestions for reading are only suggestions, and I offer them with no intention of imposing limits on either the energetic student or the resourceful teacher.

# Contents

xi

# WHAT IS PHILOSOPHY?

ONE

For joint reading with this chapter, Plato's *Euthyphro* is suggested.
It is a short dialogue about piety and is an example of the way
Socrates used philosophical method to reveal the subtleties and
contradictions in everyday notions which the unphilosophically minded
are certain to miss.

# Philosophy

This book treats philosophy as what philosophers have learned
about certain topics by using philosophical method. By its nature
the book is an illustration of philosophical method; but my
primary aim is not to write a manual on the art of philosophizing. I address myself to readers whose first interest is to learn
about philosophy. There will be time enough for them to learn
to philosophize. I must say, however, that philosophizing is not
a skill that can be picked up from a "How-to" book. Philosophy
is like the measles. It must be caught from someone who is already infected. To learn to philosophize, you must try your luck
arguing with a live philosopher. This is not to say that you
should not argue with philosophy books and try to imagine what
their authors might say in reply. Indeed, you ought to try to
argue even with this book. But to polish your skill as a philosopher, you must have a live conversationalist to oppose, criticize, and finally confirm your philosophical judgments. Philosophy is a social enterprise. If this book bothers you the way
I hope that it will, it will drive you to seek the company of a
philosopher.

## PHILOSOPHY AND PHILOSOPHICAL METHOD

The question "What is philosophy?" is like the question "What
is furniture?" Both "philosophy" and "furniture" are words that

3

can be applied to many things. To answer "What is furniture?" one must introduce the questioner to a long list of objects, of which table, chair, and bed are only the beginning. In addition, certain subsidiary questions will arise: Is a stove a piece of furniture? Is a bathtub? Is a fireplace? If I use the floor for a table, is the floor a piece of furniture? What is the difference between furniture and fixtures? Between furniture and fittings? How is the word "furniture" related to "furnished" and "unfurnished"? In short, to answer the question "What is furniture?" one must detail the different ways in which the word "furniture" may be used. Similarly, an answer to the question "What is philosophy?" requires a detailing of what the word may mean. We can do no better than to begin by considering the practice of the ancient Greeks who invented philosophy.

For the Greeks, to do philosophy was to ask two closely related questions, the skeletons of which look like this: "What is X?" and "What do you mean when you talk about X as you do?" In these question forms the X may be replaced by such words as "justice" or "the soul" or "a good state." Both these kinds of question have had lively histories and both are central to philosophy today. "What is X?" can encompass as much or as little as a philosopher likes and still remain a vehicle for knotty problems. For instance, Plato started with questions like "What is courage?" and "What is piety?" and went on to the higher level question "What is virtue?" ("Higher level" because "virtue" is more general than "courage" and "piety.") This line of thought finally led him to ask, "Is there an invisible moral order behind the visible world?"

The method the Greek philosophers used to answer the "What is X?" kind of question is epitomized in their other question, "What do you mean?" For the Greek philosophers thought that the way to find out about something is to consider what can be said about it. Plato, for example, thought that the way to find out the nature of the good was to notice the ways in which the word "good" is used. His researches led him to conclude that the way the word "good" is used to talk about many different good things implied the existence of The Good, a timeless quality, transcending the world, which all good things must imitate in their goodness, else they could not be good.

When a philosopher analyzes what someone says, he might be thought of as straining what is said through a sieve that keeps back two kinds of talk: the nonsensical and the self-contradictory. To put his task positively, he counts what people say as a clue to the nature of something when what they say both makes sense and is self-consistent. Sense and nonsense, and self-consistency and self-contradiction, are then key concepts in philosophy and it must be one of the principal tasks of this book to illustrate their use. Both sense and self-consistency may best be made clear by a consideration of their negation. It will be to the point then to discuss nonsense and self-contradiction briefly here. As we shall see, self-contradiction is one kind of nonsense.

The word "nonsense" has several different meanings, not all of which are of interest to the philosopher. For instance, Edward Lear called his rhymes "nonsense"; but they can be understood; and are, thus, not senseless. So by calling his rhymes "nonsense" Lear must have meant only that they were not to be taken seriously. We also call "nonsense" silly sounds that resemble talk but are not. However, while pig Latin sounds silly it is not senseless. We also call "nonsense" talk that makes no sense to a person because he has not learned how to understand it, although others have. For example, there are many passages in chemistry books which are nonsense to me; but in principle they will make sense to anyone who will go through the training requisite to understanding them. The Jabberwocky sentence " 'Twas brillig, and the slithy toves/ Did gyre and gimble in the wabe" did not make sense to Alice until Humpty Dumpty, who could understand it, explained it.

The meanings of "nonsense" which are of interest to philosophers are these two: A piece of talk might not make sense to someone because it has not yet been given a sense; and a piece of talk might not make sense to someone because it is self-contradictory and cannot be given a sense. An example of talk that has not yet been given a sense is one discussed by Moritz

Schlick: "Take me to a country where the sky is three times as
blue as in England." [1] This command makes no sense because
we do not now have a method for measuring the blueness of
skies. But if such a method were invented, we could give sense
to the command and assess the possibility of carrying it out. The
philosopher's impulse to give a sense to talk that would apparently be senseless without his efforts has been the source of much
philosophy. For example, much of what philosophers have had
to say about God, the soul, immortality, and material substance
has its origin here.

The second sort of nonsense which I have said is of interest
to philosophers is talk which does not make sense because it is
self-contradictory and cannot be given a sense. A prime case of
self-contradiction is any statement of the form "X is not X,"
provided that the word which replaces the X is used in the same
sense each time. But a self-contradictory statement need not be
made in this immediately obvious form. Consider, for example,
"Quadrilaterals have six sides." If the statement means that four-
sided figures have six sides, and "side" is being used in the same
sense in all instances, then the statement is a self-contradiction.
A figure completely defined by its four sides cannot have six
sides.

A good example of the place in philosophical method of attention to self-contradiction is to be found in philosophers' interest in the statement "Nothing can come from nothing." They
hold this statement to be true because the statement "Something
can come from nothing" is a patent self-contradiction. They
argue then that there must be something which is the ever-exist-
ing source of all that is, for, as they have shown, nothing can
come from nothing. This argument is regularly used as a decisive step in proving either that everything in the world must
have originated from a prime stuff or that everything must have
originated from God.

[1] From his essay "Meaning and Verification," reprinted in *Readings in Philosophical Analysis*, ed. by Feigl and Sellars (New York, Appleton-Century-Crofts),
1949.

## PHILOSOPHY AND NATURAL SCIENCE

The study of sense and consistency, of nonsense and self-contradiction, belongs to logic, the science of sound arguments; and the philosopher's method may be said to be the method of logic. Knowing something of that method, we are now in a position to throw a little more light on the question "What is philosophy?" by contrasting philosophy with the natural sciences. Such a contrast is important to us because it may be said that natural scientists (physicists, chemists, astronomers, geologists, and biologists, for example) also ask and answer the question "What is X?" The easy distinction to make between philosophy and natural science seems to be to say that philosophy tells us what there is by means of logic and natural science tells us what there is by means of observation. Alas, there is some justice in this easy answer. For too often, as we shall see, philosophers have announced the ultimate nature of the world on the basis of logic, without trying to confirm their description of the world by observation. Regrettably for the fate of many philosophers, an infinite number of worlds is logically possible; and while the one in which we live must be logically describable, its actual identification is finally a matter of observation. But it must be added that, even though philosophers' pronouncements may sometimes be the fruit of logic without observation, natural science cannot be observation without logic. For one cannot start looking for something unless one can conceive in some degree what it is one is looking for. The notions of sense and consistency are central to the task of scientific conception. A striking example of the connection between philosophical method and natural science is to be found in Einstein's analysis of the meaning of "simultaneity" as a preface to his theory of relativity. Einstein pointed out that when we say two events, each in a different place, happen simultaneously, any measure of their simultaneity is relative to the location of the observer appointed to watch for them. There is no absolute time scale, functioning independently of all observers, on which to measure simultaneity. Einstein's theory of relativity then grows out of his analysis of what we mean when we say that two events happen simultaneously.[2]

Another way of bringing out the difference between philosophy and the natural sciences is to argue that these sciences are tame philosophy. Philosophy as a method is a critique of claims to know what there is. A philosopher's line of attack goes like this: Let us be clear about what it is that we are talking about. When we have achieved clarity, we shall know what tests we can make to find out whether or not what we are talking about exists. Agreement about the nature and investigatibility of any subject depends on the success of this philosophical search for clarity. Now, for any subject, when there comes to be agreement about what it is that is being discussed and about what methods are to be used in answering questions about the subject, a science is born.

Physics, the oldest of the natural sciences, provides a dramatic example of what I am talking about. Physics, as speculation about motion or change in the world, had a long history before the time of Galileo (1564-1642). But there was little agreement about the kind of motion or change a physicist should be studying. Should he study the abstract concept of change itself? Or should he study the movement of particular bodies through space? Or should he study biological growth? What is more, should he go beyond the various instances of change and endeavor to deduce the nature of the world, divine or otherwise, that makes change possible? Galileo's gift to physics was to transform it from a philosophical subject to a science. He initiated the program that physics should be the study of the motion or change in inanimate bodies. In addition, he defined the conditions for carrying on the science. The physicist was to be limited to the *observation* of the measurable qualities of bodies in motion, and the consequent *description* of their behavior in generalizations which could be stated as mathematical formulae. No speculation about the place in physics of such unobservable and indescribable entities as God and his angels was to be allowed.

[2] See Albert Einstein, *Relativity, the Special and the General Theory, A Popular Exposition* (London, Methuen), 1920, Chapters VIII and IX.

No attempt was to be made to describe any quality of a body which could not be measured and its quantity expressed mathematically. Galileo's success in prescribing his way of doing physics to other physicists is to be explained by the impressiveness of his discoveries. Had his views on the questions physicists ought to ask and the methods they ought to use in answering them not enabled him to make remarkable and interesting discoveries, he would have been but another passing shadow in the history of physical speculation.

Even though sciences may be described as tame philosophy, a science may still have its wildly philosophical part. For the establishment of a science is a matter of degree. Agreement among the students of a particular science is necessary only about some of the questions to be asked and only about some of the methods for answering them. The degree to which a subject is a science can be measured by the amount of agreement there is among its students about questions and methods for answering them. But the answering of old questions may suggest new questions, which may require new methods for finding answers. The philosophical part of a science is that part in which its practitioners are debating the intelligibility of new questions and scrutinizing the proposed methods for answering them.

It follows from this account of the sciences as tame philosophy that the truly philosophical subjects are subjects about whose nature philosophers still disagree, and as a consequence there is little agreement about methods for studying these subjects. But the very fact that there is much disagreement about the nature of a subject may tell us something important about that subject. It may be a subject on which no one view is more plausible than another and each philosopher is entitled to form his own opinion without expecting everyone else to agree. What we can expect of philosophers is an account of their grounds for holding the views they do about philosophical subjects. The evaluation of these grounds, if they can be evaluated, is one of the central problems of philosophy, and difference of opinion about their evaluation is one of the chief causes of different schools of philosophy.

## PHILOSOPHY AND RELIGION

A little more light will be thrown on the question "What is philosophy?" by comparing philosophy and religion. Both the religious and the philosophical take an interest in describing the ultimate nature of reality. In respect to subject matter, the writings of the principal Greek philosophers, Plato and Aristotle, are indistinguishable from religion. For Plato, philosophy is the search for The Good, which is the source of the moral order. For Aristotle, philosophy proves the existence of the Prime Mover, who is the source of the physical order. Both The Good and the Prime Mover are entities which the monotheist who reads philosophy is inclined to identify as God. The difference between philosophy and religion, at least as Jews, Christians, and Muslims understand it, then, is in the contrast between method in philosophy and revelation in religion. To the philosopher, the ultimate nature of reality is discoverable through the use of human powers by anyone who has the intellect, energy, and perseverance to seek. But for the religious person, God, who is the ultimate reality, may be sought by anyone, but he is found only when he chooses to reveal himself. God's grace, not human persistence, explains the success of any religious quest. In contrast with religion then, philosophy is squarely for the use of human powers to know what can be known. There is nothing hidden to be noticed only when it chooses to reveal itself. Whatever is, is discoverable; and nothing else is. A certain kind of religious person, the natural theologian, has, however, tried to use philosophical method to establish religious truths; and I shall examine these efforts at length in a later chapter.

## YOUR PHILOSOPHY OF LIFE

Another way of answering the question "What is philosophy?" is to say that someone's philosophy is the principles by which he conducts his life. His principles are his philosophy of life. This book cannot give you a philosophy of life. Nor can a philosopher give you a philosophy of life. You may make someone else's philosophy your own, or you may make your own philosophy; but the making can only be your own doing. This book will introduce you to philosophers' conclusions about what is valuable in the world and in human life. But even after you know philosophers' opinions about what is valuable, you must still decide for yourself whether you are to agree with any one of them. What this book can do is to acquaint you with great questions which you may never before have thought of asking. Or if you have thought of the questions, this book may acquaint you with answers which you have not yet considered. But the answers you finally accept must be answers which you have made your own.

The philosophical enterprise is in many respects mankind's greatest ornament. Philosophy is both a critique of human powers and an effort to use those powers to understand the world and to lead a good life. It is the philosopher's claim that by human powers alone man can come to terms with the world and find happiness. Some philosophers have exalted one human power to the exclusion of others. The intellect, faith, reason, the senses, innumerable passions and appetites, and even sheer physical durability, each has had its partisans. But whatever the power emphasized, it has been claimed that man could use this power to make his own way in the world. No philosopher has ever claimed that mankind has exhausted the possibilities of human powers in the effort to capture happiness. The claim is not that no human power will avail mankind, but that what is needed is a greater use of human powers.

## SUGGESTIONS FOR FURTHER READING

Two short accounts of philosophers' lives which show the interests of philosophers and their devotion to their calling are the *Apology* by Plato, a report of Socrates' speeches at his trial, in which he defends his practice of philosophy, and the *Discourse on Method* by René Descartes, which is both Descartes's philosophical autobiography and an exposition of the method which led him to his philosophical conclusions.

There are three books which are amusing not only in themselves but doubly so when they are read as both illustrations and criticisms of philosophical method. They are *Alice in Wonderland* and *Through the Looking Glass* by Lewis Carroll, and *Many Moons* by James Thurber (Harcourt, Brace, New York, 1943).

## TWO

For joint reading with this chapter, *An Inquiry Concerning Human Understanding* by David Hume, Section IV, "Sceptical Doubts Concerning the Operations of the Understanding," is suggested. There Hume discusses his division of the objects of human reason into matters of fact and relations of ideas, the latter of which are called in this chapter "matters of logic."

# *Philosophy and Man: Intellectual Powers*

In this chapter I shall discuss man's powers to know and the kinds of knowledge which these powers guarantee. The discussion will center on two kinds of knowledge: matters of fact, which depend on man's senses, or his powers of perceiving; and matters of logic, which depend on man's reason, or his powers of conceiving. This chapter is a necessary preface to all the rest. If what is said here seems formal, empty, and uninteresting, I must beg the reader to remember that until we settle questions about the *ways* in which we can know, we cannot settle questions about *what* we can know. This is one of the central problems in philosophy, and one to which philosophers turn again and again as the key to all of their other problems.

In what follows I shall consider knowledge as declarative sentences or statements, which someone knows how to prove or to use. There is more than one way of proving and using declarative sentences, but the example of the Pythagorean Theorem will illustrate my point in a general way. The theorem: "In any right-angled triangle, the square which is described on the side opposite the right angle is equal to the squares described on the sides which contain the right angle." Now I may be said to know the theorem when I can prove it by appeal to the necessary definitions, postulates, axioms, and preceding theorems in Euclidean geometry, when I can use it to prove further theorems, and when I can use it to find the length of unknown sides, and so on.

Knowledge may also be spoken of as knowing some object. For example, philosophers like to talk about our knowledge of material objects; and they like to talk in general about objects of knowledge. But talk about objects of knowledge can always be translated into talk about knowing whether a statement about the object is true or false. The reader will find it a salutary move to translate an awesome question like "Can I really know material objects?" into the more manageable question, "How do I know that the statement, 'There is a tea cup on my desk,' is true?" What is more, talk about knowledge as statements puts us in a favorable position to deal with the social aspect of knowledge. Whatever my object of knowledge, if I want to call someone's attention to it or to discuss it with him, I must make statements about it. Statements are the medium for exchanging knowledge; and this consideration makes them additionally interesting as a clue to man's powers to know.

## MATTER-OF-FACT STATEMENTS

We may begin with matter-of-fact statements, and see what can be made of them in their own right. Later, when we have also examined matter-of-logic statements, we may consider the differences between the two kinds of statement. Here are some sample matter-of-fact statements:

> The cows are in the corn field.
> Alice always talks too much.
> The sun will rise tomorrow.
> Aristotle gave philosophy lectures.
> Alexander swam the Hellespont.
> The Eiffel Tower is in New York City.

These statements differ in many ways. All are about different subjects. Some are in the present tense, while others are about the past and the future. Some are statements about a particular subject at a particular time. Some are generalizations about a particular subject, and thus are meant to describe that subject at all times (e.g. Alice always talks too much). But despite their many differences, the characteristic which these statements have in common is that they may be proved true or false by experience.

It is easy to say that matter-of-fact statements are confirmed or disproved by experience; but it is not easy to give any general account of what is meant by experience. What is usually meant is that someone who wants to confirm a matter-of-fact statement must use his senses in some way to find out whether the statement does describe the world. When we find that a matter-of-fact statement does describe the world, we say that it is confirmed. When we find that a matter-of-fact statement fails to describe the world, we say that it is disproved. Here, we may consider the following examples which are meant to illustrate in a general way the confirmation of a matter-of-fact statement by experience.

(1) When someone tells me, "The cows are in the corn field," I look in the corn field to see whether I can find the cows there. If they are in the corn field, my finding them there has confirmed the statement. My failing to find them in the corn field would disprove it. But I must not minimize the difficulties in proving this statement false, or, to put the matter another way, the difficulties in proving that the statement "The cows are not in the corn field" is true. To be sure, I must have searched, and searched carefully. Of course, looking for cows in a corn field requires less care than hunting for a needle in a haystack; but nonetheless I must be certain that I have looked in all those places big enough to conceal a herd of cows before I can assert confidently that there are no cows in the corn field in question. The proof of the affirmative statement "The cows are in the corn field" is, however, fairly easy. All I have to do is find the cows. But the proof of the negative statement is more difficult. No matter how exhaustive a search I conduct before I conclude that the cows are not in the corn field, it is still possible that they might be hidden in a spot that I have missed.

(2) While riding with me in my car, someone tells me, "The radiator is boiling." I can neither see nor hear anything unusual from the direction of the radiator; so I look at the temperature gauge. If the indicator is in the red section of its arc, I agree with my passenger. His statement is true. But here confirmation by experience is more complicated than in the case above, where I looked into the corn field and saw the cows. Why does my seeing the temperature indicator in the red section prove true the statement "The radiator is boiling"? It proves it for me because I believe another statement, which links the behavior of the indicator and the behavior of the radiator: "If the indicator is in the red, the radiator is boiling." And why do I believe this last statement? I believe it because in the past each time the indicator has gone into the red section of its arc, I have found the car's radiator to be boiling. So now when I find the indicator in the red I believe that the radiator must be boiling.

But one may very well ask why my memory of the indicator's riding in the red when the radiator was boiling in the past in any way guarantees that my radiator is now boiling because the indicator is riding in the red section. Strictly speaking, there is no guarantee that there is now a connection between the position of the indicator and my radiator's boiling. Matter-of-fact statements are meant to describe the world, and it is possible that the world may have changed since I last experienced a link between the position of the indicator and the radiator's boiling. My temperature gauge may now be broken, to name the most probable way in which the world may have changed. But even though there is no guarantee that there is a connection between the position of the indicator and my radiator's boiling, it usually happens in cases of this kind that our belief that the present resembles the past outweighs our knowledge that the world may have changed. Our belief about a particular kind of connection grows stronger each time we experience it. On the other hand, those occasions when experience disproves our matter-of-fact statements (The gauge was broken. The radiator was not even hot.) are salutary reminders that matter-of-fact statements are meant to describe the world rather than to prescribe it.

(3) "The sun will rise tomorrow" is yet another and different example of a statement that we say is true because of experience. But here there is no present experience comparable to looking at an indicator in the red portion of its arc, that leads from the seen to belief in the unseen. It is the regularity of our past experience of sunrises that leads us to expect that the sun will rise tomorrow, and thus leads us to say that the statement is true. Of course, neither my past experience of sunrises nor the expectation it engenders makes the statement true. Only the sun's rising on the morrow can do that.

These three examples show that confirmation of a matter-of-fact statement by experience may have at least these three meanings: (1) I am directly observing what the statement describes, and what I observe justifies my saying that the statement is true. (2) I am directly observing one thing, which I have regularly found to be conjoined with the state of affairs described by the statement, and this observation leads me to believe that the state of affairs which the statement describes, but which I have not observed, does exist; and I say that the statement is true. In principle we argue for the truth of statements about the past or the future in the same way when we say that what we can see implies the existence of past events which we have not seen or when we argue that what we can see implies the probability of events yet to come. (3) I remember something that I have regularly observed in the past; and I am led to believe that a similar state of affairs which the statement describes, but which I have not yet observed, will exist; and I say that the statement is true.

To these remarks about confirming by experience must be added the rule that no one can confirm a matter-of-fact statement who does not know what observations will confirm it. If I do not know the difference between cows and the rest of the world, and corn fields and the rest of the world, the statement "The corn field is in the cows" will make as much sense to me as the statement "The cows are in the corn field." Philosophers say that someone who does not know how to confirm a matter-of-fact statement does not understand it. To him, it is meaning-less. To him, it makes no sense.

After this consideration of proving and disproving matter-of-fact statements, we are in a position to notice one of their characteristics that is their defining characteristic. For every matter-of-fact statement, its denial is as meaningful as the statement itself. For instance, "The cows are not in the corn field" is as meaningful as "The cows are in the corn field." It is because each is as meaningful as the other that we must appeal to experience to determine which is true. Later we shall find this characteristic to be of the greatest importance in distinguishing matter-of-fact statements from matter-of-logic statements.

## THE SENSES AND KNOWLEDGE

Matter-of-fact statements are the kind of knowledge we may gain by the use of our senses; but not all philosophers have thought that our senses are fit instruments for gaining knowledge of the world. Their views deserve some notice. At the outset, however, I wish to announce that I am not claiming that the only knowledge we have is knowledge confirmed by our senses. Therefore, neither does the position I am describing hold its place by belittling other sources of knowledge, nor does it deserve belittlement for the purpose of enhancing other sources of knowledge.

The criticism of the senses as powers for knowing falls under two main heads: the claim that the fallibility of the senses makes all sensory knowledge untrustworthy; and the claim that the senses can never be used to gain knowledge of the real world.

The claim that the senses are fallible rests on evidence that the senses deceive. The classic examples fall into two varieties: the failure to perceive things as they are, and the mistake of perceiving things that are not. Examples of the failure to perceive things as they are, are the straight stick that looks bent in water; the penny at one's feet that turns out to be a bottle cap; the mountain that seems quite near but turns out to be a hundred miles away; the man in the night who turns out to be a windblown bush; and the burglar's footsteps that turn into a dripping faucet. The problems in these examples arise largely from assuming more than the sensory evidence warrants. The fault lies not with the senses but with the hasty assumption; and its avoidance lies not in abandoning the senses because they are untrustworthy, but in seeking more sensory knowledge to confirm or disprove one's first assumption. What is more, as soon as one learns the tricks one's senses can play, one learns to be careful in judging water effects, distance, and shadows.

But if we pursue the fallibility of the senses a little further, we discover that a good part of the trouble comes from personifying the senses: from my thinking of my use of my senses as a communication between *me* and my senses. I say, "My eyes deceived me," when I ought to say, "*I* should have taken another look." I say, "My ears tricked me," when I ought to say, "*I* should have listened more carefully." I say, "My nose knows," when I ought to say, "*I* smell it." The problem of the fallibility of the senses turns into the problem of the careless observer when we make ourselves the subject of verbs of sense. Then we know that we have only ourselves to blame for our perceptual mistakes. Ordinary people know this; but philosophers have to be reminded from time to time.

The mistake of perceiving things that are not is exemplified by mirages, unrecognized mirror images, and the one-legged man who still feels rheumatic pains in his amputated member. The solution of the problems raised by these examples requires again a greater use of the senses. Three tests are possible: the test of two or more observers; the test of observations at different times; and the test of two or more senses. Do I see an oasis or do I see a mirage? If I can see it at different times, and if my fellow travelers can see it at the same times I do, my answer is a tentative "Oasis." Tentative, because the test of an optical experience is, can I touch what I see? It may be objected, of course, that sensory tests are circular. Touch confirms sight, and sight confirms touch. One illusion leads to another, and all is illusion. This objection leads us to the second main head under which criticism of the senses is made: The senses can never be used to gain knowledge of the real world.

"Real" is a loaded word. If it is used to describe a world that transcends the powers of our senses, then by definition we can never learn anything of that world by our senses. But here I understand the denial of sensory knowledge of a real world to be a claim that the world is a creation of one's senses, and that one cannot tell what to credit to the world and what to attribute to one's senses. The claim is that the knower and his knowledge run together indistinguishably.

The distinction between the knower and the known is not always an easy one to make; and it often depends on where the philosopher wants to draw the line. Consider, for example, the Wizard of Oz and his Emerald City. To achieve the absolute greenness of Oz, the Wizard equipped all of his subjects and visitors with green spectacles, which they were compelled to wear at all times. Now here is a nice philosophical question: Was the city of Oz really green or was its greenness merely in the eyes of its beholders? (Said eyes being properly assisted by green spectacles, of course.) Whether or not a philosopher says that Oz was really green depends on where he draws the line between the beholders and the world. If the philosopher says that Oz was really not green, he is ready to argue that if the inhabitants had taken off their colored spectacles, they would have found the city to be not wholly green. Such a philosopher is answering the question from a viewpoint above the relation of the beholder to the city; and thus he finds green not in the world but in the eye of the beholder. On the other hand, a philosopher might argue that the question about Oz's greenness must always be answered from within the relationship of the beholder and the world. For such a philosopher, when someone says, "Oz isn't really green," he is only saying, "I am not looking at Oz through green spectacles." So, from the point of view of those subject to the Wizard's spectacles, Oz is really green.

The philosophical moral is that only when we can distinguish between two different ways of knowing the world (without green spectacles and with green spectacles) are we in any position to distinguish between what is the world and what is a condition for knowing the world. Without the correction of other perceptions—in the way that clear-eyed observers can penetrate the Wizard of Oz's color-scheming—the world of sense is as real as we perceive it. There is some truth in saying that we are the prisoners of our senses; but we may take consolation in the fact that our prison is not a cave-like dungeon, but a house of correction.

## MATTER-OF-LOGIC STATEMENTS

I want now to turn to matter-of-logic statements. As always, it will be best to proceed by way of examples:

> The whole is equal to the sum of its parts.
> In any right-angled triangle the square which is described on the side opposite the right angle is equal to the squares described on the sides which contain the right angle. (Pythagorean Theorem)
> Three times five is equal to one-half of thirty.
> That which is red is colored.

Why do we accept or reject these statements? In a general way, the answer is that matter-of-logic statements are confirmed by an appeal to the way in which we use the words in the statement. How does this sort of confirmation work? I shall illustrate it by considering "The whole is equal to the sum of its parts."

In the case of "The whole is equal to the sum of its parts," the appeal is to the way in which we are to use the words "whole," "part," and "equal to" in this statement. That into which a whole can be divided is its parts. That into which parts can be assembled is a whole. Further, there is a question of the kind of whole that we will allow this statement to describe. The rough rule is that the wholes and their parts must be subject to some system of measurement as of area or weight or volume. What "equal to" means in "The whole is equal to the sum of its parts" is that whatever quantitative measurement can be applied to the whole can also be applied to the sum of the parts. Now the confirmation of "The whole is equal to the sum of its parts" depends solely on my understanding the way in which these words are to be used and by agreeing to use them in this way. This is why I call such a statement a matter-of-logic statement, for our "logic" comes from the Greek *logos* meaning "word." In addition, I must digress for a moment to give a little historical perspective to what I have spoken of as "understanding the way in which words are to be used." For a very long time, philosophers thought about matter-of-logic statements as being about ideas or concepts rather than about words. This was their way of distinguishing between matter-of-fact statements, which were about perceptions, and matter-of-logic statements, which were about conceptions. In addition, just as perceptions were perceived by the senses, so a faculty called reason was thought of as conceiving conceptions, or ideas. Thus many philosophers speak of confirming matter-of-logic statements as an appeal to reason; but I want to follow those philosophers who speak of confirming matter-of-logic statements as reminding ourselves of the ways in which we may use these statements.

We can carry our understanding of matter-of-logic statements a little further if we consider the way in which we use "The whole is equal to the sum of its parts." This matter-of-logic statement is really a rule which allows me the convenience of mentioning the whole rather than listing all of the parts. For example, when you ask me how much money I have, I can tell you that I have two dollars and thirty-six cents rather than having to say that I have three nickels, two dimes, a penny, two quarters, and three half-dollars. But notice that the confirmation of "The whole is equal to the sum of its parts" never depends on any example of its usefulness. I do not say that the statement is true because my pocketful of coins is the same as two dollars and thirty-six cents. I say that the statement is true because I understand the way in which the words are used. On the other hand, I never allow that any example can disprove the statement either. My tactics are to show that any example which someone believes disproves "The whole is equal to the sum of its parts" is really not a case to which the rule can be applied; and anyone who supposes that it is such a case misunderstands the way in which the rule is to be used. An example will illustrate my point.

Suppose that someone argues in the following way: I can show you that the whole is not equal to the sum of its parts. Look at this medicine dropper full of liquid. Now, I squeeze it ten times, and let ten drops fall into this saucer; and they run together to make one drop. That shows you that the whole is not equal to the sum of its parts, for the sum of the parts is ten drops, but the whole in the saucer is only one drop.

My reply to this argument must be that I am being taken in a numbers game. When I said that the whole is equal to the sum of its parts, I never meant to claim that one is equal to ten. Indeed, enumerative equality is not the sort of equality which can be sought between a whole and its parts, since the whole will always be one, and the number of its parts will always be greater than one. What has happened is that the drops case has been presented in such a way that it does not fit the rule. So it can in no way disprove my claim that the whole is equal to the sum of its parts. I can, however, turn the example to my own account by showing how it can be made to fit the rule. I can talk about the volume of the drop in the saucer and the volume of the ten drops that were squeezed from the medicine dropper. When their volume is considered, the whole is equal to the sum of the parts. What is required here is discretion in summing. Notice, however, that by showing how the drops case can be made to fit the rule, I am not appealing to the case to confirm the matter-of-logic statement, "The whole is equal to the sum of its parts." What I am doing is showing a case in which the rule can be used.

I now want to distinguish two sorts of matter-of-logic statements. The sorts which I have in mind are exemplified by "That which is red is colored," and the Pythagorean Theorem. To bring out their characteristics, I shall discuss each of these statements in turn. Notice that the statement, "That which is red is colored," is always true, for its denial, "That which is red is NOT colored," is a self-contradiction, granting that as we ordinarily use the color word "red," to say that something is red is to say that it is colored. For the same reason, of course, the self-contradictory statement, "Red objects are NOT colored," will always be false.

Now consider the Pythagorean Theorem, which I wish to discuss because it exemplifies those matter-of-logic statements which are part of a logical system of statements, as that theorem is a part of Euclidean geometry. It is the case that this sort of matter-of-logic statement is also always true; indeed it is this characteristic which leads us to classify these statements, too, as matter-of-logic statements. However, these statements are not said to be always true because their denials are self-contradictory, as is the case with "That which is red is colored." A longer explanation is required. We say that the Pythagorean Theorem is true because we can prove it within the context of Euclidean geometry. We appeal to the relevant definitions, postulates, and axioms laid down in the beginning, and to any relevant theorems that were proved earlier, and our claim is that all of these taken together imply the truth of the Pythagorean Theorem. The principle of our proof is that we can show the Pythagorean Theorem to be consistent with the rest of Euclidean geometry. If we then counted it as false, we should be contradicting ourselves, in the light of our adherence to the rest of Euclidean geometry. Valuing self-consistency, we therefore count the Pythagorean Theorem as true and its denial as false. Could its denial ever be true? Yes, if we invented an alternative geometry into which it could fit; and that such a geometry is conceivable is what makes us refrain from calling the denial of the Pythagorean Theorem a self-contradiction. We only say that within Euclidean geometry it cannot be true.

There is another way to bring out the reason for classifying both "Red objects are colored" and the Pythagorean Theorem as matter-of-logic statements. It is that we disallow the denial of each for a logical reason: in the first case because it is a self-contradiction and in the second because of inconsistency with our original principles. We may then formulate rules for detecting each of the different sorts of matter-of-logic statement. The first is that if a statement's denial is a self-contradiction, then it is a matter-of-logic statement. The second is that if the assertion of a statement's denial is disallowed because of its inconsistency with the logical system of statements into which the statement itself fits, then it is a matter-of-logic statement. Notice that if the application of one rule is inconclusive, the other must be applied before one can be satisfied about whether a given statement belongs in the matter-of-logic category.

We may now notice another characteristic of matter-of-logic statements. They do not describe the world. Consider, for example, "That which is red is colored." The statement makes no claim that there is anything red in the world. It is only an assertion that if there are red things in the world, then they are colored. But even though matter-of-logic statements do not describe the world, they may have a great deal to do with the way in which we look at the world. Consider, for example, the usefulness of "The whole is equal to the sum of its parts," a matter-of-logic statement I have already discussed. We do not want to say that this statement describes the world in the sense that it can be confirmed or disproved by experience. But in our use of the statement it is clearly not unrelated to experience, for we do order appropriate parts of our experiences in accordance with it. This is not to say, however, that all matter-of-logic statements are, or need to be, useful in the ordering of experience. For instance, many geometries have been invented simply because of the charm which their elegant self-consistency has exercised on the minds of their inventors; and no thought is given to the question of whether they describe any discoverable space.

## MATTERS OF FACT AND LOGIC

From what I have written thus far, my readers may suppose that all statements come neatly labeled "matter-of-fact" or "matter-of-logic," and there can be no trouble in deciding into which basket a given statement should be sorted. Unfortunately this orderly picture is inaccurate, and the kind of puzzle about which a philosopher is most likely to work his head to the bone is one generated by the ins and outs of classifying some statement. There are, however, ways of testing statements that help to decide whether they are to be classified as matter-of-fact or matter-of-logic. I have already described the rules for testing for matter-of-logic statements. I want now to show how points made earlier provide a test for identifying matter-of-fact statements.

Consider the statement, "My collar button is on the bureau." Now even though my collar button is on the bureau, and thus the statement is true, I know what it would be like for its denial, "My collar button is NOT on the bureau," to be true. As I have described things, the denial is, of course, false; but notice that if I did not know how to find out the truth of both statements, I could not find out the truth of either. To find that my collar button is on the bureau, I must also know what it would be like for it not to be on the bureau, or else how could I start looking for it? Should the reader doubt what I have said, he may set himself the task of finding out the truth of the statement, "There is a xonygl in the next room." His first question must be, "What is a xonygl?" If he does not know how to tell the difference between xonygls and everything else in the next room, he is in no position to check on the presence of xonygls. Philosophers like to speak of this as knowing the difference between xonygls and non-xonygls. When someone knows this difference, he will be able to find out the truth of either "There is a xonygl in the next room" or "There is NOT a xonygl in the next room."

The denials of matter-of-fact statements, then, may be either true or false, and a look at the world is required in order to decide whether a given matter-of-fact statement or its denial is true. Here, then, is our test for matter-of-fact statements: Their denials are as conceivable as the original statements, and we can decide which is true only by an appeal to experience. Here too is a basis for our distinction between matter-of-fact and matter-of-logic statements. The denial of the first sort of matter-of-logic statement we noticed is inconceivable because it is a self-contradiction; and the denial of the second sort is not to be allowed because it is inconsistent with the logical system of statements into which the original statement fits.

These distinctions are neatly stated; but they are not the end of the matter. The tangle of fact and logic is such that there are some statements which we sometimes allow to be matter-of-fact and at other times count as matter-of-logic. It would seem that our distinctions depend not only on the outcome of our tests, but also on which test we want to make. It remains to make this state of affairs as clear as it can be made in a small space and without long practice on the reader's part.

Is "My orange is segmented" a matter-of-fact or a matter-of-logic statement? Orange segments are those pieces into which the inner membrane naturally divides the pulp. Now, is its denial, "My orange is NOT segmented," conceivable? Can we say what we should have to find, in order to say that the statement is true? I think so. A non-segmented orange would have no inner membrane, so that the pulp would be undifferentiated, as in peaches. Notice that it does seem that if we did not know how to tell the difference between being segmented and being non-segmented, we could not discover the truth of either "My orange is segmented" or its denial. Since we can conceive its denial, we must put this statement in the matter-of-fact basket.

But at this point, someone might ask this puzzling question: "Would you call that object you are eating an orange if it were not segmented?" I am being squeezed to decide whether "My orange is segmented" *must* be either matter-of-fact or matter-of-logic. If I answer "Yes," then the statement could be true or false and it is matter-of-fact. If I answer "No," the statement is being made to work like a definition. It is, therefore, always true, and must be counted as a matter-of-logic statement. Let us consider this "No" answer a little more.

When I say that I would not consider the object I am eating an orange if it were not segmented, I am agreeing to a rule for defining oranges: "If it is an orange, then it is segmented." Having agreed to such a rule, I must say either, "My orange is segmented," or nothing at all. Clearly I cannot say, "My orange is not segmented," for that is a self-contradictory statement. How do these considerations help me to decide whether my statement is matter-of-fact or matter-of-logic? It should now be clear that my decision depends on how I decide that I am using the statement. This is what I meant earlier when I said that we must not only apply the tests for distinguishing matter-of-fact and matter-of-logic statements, we must also decide what test is to be made. If I say that I am describing my orange when I say, "My orange is segmented," then the test can be applied to discover that the statement is matter-of-fact. If I say that I am speaking in accordance with the botanical definition of "orange" when I say, "My orange is segmented," then the test can be applied to discover that the statement is matter-of-logic.

We may finish by noticing what the classification of statements has to do with the limits of human knowledge. Philosophers have claimed that whatever is knowledge is expressible in either a matter-of-fact or a matter-of-logic statement. It must be admitted that this claim is open to challenge; but it is such a fundamental characteristic of philosophy that it is seldom challenged. Indeed, it is extremely difficult to imagine the terms in which a challenge could be stated. To carry the argument, one would have to convince a philosopher either that he has a cognitive power beyond the usual ones of perception and conception, or at the very least that there are people who have this new power and that he can be convinced of its existence as certainly as he can be convinced of the difference between blind and sighted persons. But convincing a philosopher that a hitherto unknown human power exists, when it is the case both that to appreciate the power he would have to exercise it or perceive it exercised, and that he denies that it is present to be exercised, appears to be an insuperable task. The little more that I can say on this point is that radical disagreement with the claim that whatever is knowledge is expressible in either matter-of-fact or matter-of-logic statements is most apt to occur when someone is caught in a violent disagreement over how the principle is to be applied, and no other way of saving his knowledge claim appears open to him except the invention of new ways of knowing and of new kinds of knowledge.

Within the limits of knowledge recognized by philosophy, then, philosophers' debates are over whether a given matter is a matter of fact or a matter of logic; and these are the debates which we shall overhear as we consider what philosophers tell us that we can know about the world, gods, human freedom, morals, and politics.

What is at stake in these debates? Most philosophers are ready to distinguish between what is in the world and what is in my mind. If something counts as a matter of fact, it exists in the world. If something counts as a matter of logic, it exists in a mind as a concept or, as I should prefer to say, as someone's knowing how to use a word. But in the history of philosophy a premium has been put on showing that something is a matter of fact, that it affects us because it is in the world and not just a concept in the mind. Thus, philosophical debates are hottest between those philosophers who want to make certain entries in the list of what there is in the world and other philosophers who do not want to let them get away with it.

### SUGGESTIONS FOR FURTHER READING

Theories of knowledge and metaphysics are closely related; so the subject of this chapter slides into that of the next, and books mentioned here are often relevant to the discussions in the next chapter. The views which Hume expresses in his *An Inquiry Concerning Human Understanding* are criticized by Immanuel Kant in his *Prolegomena to Any Future Metaphysics*. The Kant is tough going. Kant's subject, the place of matter-of-logic statements in our knowledge of the world, is discussed with modern thoroughness by Professor C. I. Lewis in his *Mind and the World-Order* (Dover). Chapter VIII "The Nature of the A Priori and the Pragmatic Element in Knowledge" is especially relevant here. See also *Language, Truth and Logic* by Professor A. J. Ayer, Chapter IV "The A Priori" (Dover).

# THREE

The following books are suggested for joint reading with this
chapter: *Republic* by Plato; *Principles of Human Knowledge*
by George Berkeley, an example of Idealist philosophy; *An
Inquiry Concerning Human Understanding* by David Hume,
an example of empiricist philosophy.

## *Philosophy and the World*

Philosophers try to understand the world as a whole. They go
about this task by trying to draw up lists of the fundamental
kinds of things the world can contain. Some lists are quite short.
Others are of a more generous length. In general the clue which
a philosopher follows in drawing up his list is his view of man's
powers to know. From it he infers the kinds of things that can
be known; and these he analyzes into their simplest and most
universal characteristics. These characteristics make up the philosopher's list of the fundamental kinds of things the world can
contain. Such a list is called a metaphysics. Just what a metaphysics can be like will become clear in the discussions that follow.

### THE PLATONIST'S WORLD

Plato's is the earliest philosophical world view to survive with
sufficient completeness to make study interesting and criticism
possible. Therefore much of later philosophy is either a develop-
ment of Plato's views or an attack on them. So this chapter begins with Plato, not because he said the last word on the nature
of the world, but because he said some first words which must
be regularly taken into account by those who want to know what
philosophy is.

The topic from Plato's philosophy which I shall discuss is his Theory of Ideas. Any consideration of that theory must begin with a respectful nod in the direction of the historical record. Plato's writings are rich in philosophical invention, but they are by no means a consistent statement of a single viewpoint. So, while an account of the Theory of Ideas may be drawn from Plato's writings, we must remember that Plato's statement of the theory leaves much to be desired and that there is no certainty that it is his final philosophical position. Indeed, he published criticisms of the theory, to which he offered no answer. Plato, then, is an admirable example of the philosopher who tries out theories for what they are worth. Only his followers have been so doctrinaire as to be Platonists, that is, unfailing adherents to the Theory of Ideas. But that theory is far from being the only item of interest in Plato's writings; and, indeed, disposing of it clears the way for discovering the richness of his views and methods. But the fact remains that the Theory of Ideas can be drawn from his writings; and no matter how uncertain we may be of the value Plato put on the theory, some of his successors have set great store by it.

Stated baldly, the Theory of Ideas claims that there exists above and beyond the world of sensible objects a world of suprasensible objects which are the ideal forms of sensible objects. Hence, the Theory of Ideas may also be referred to as the Theory of Forms. The classic example offered to explicate the theory is known as "Plato's bed." There is an ideal bed laid up in heaven; and all beds in the sensible world here below resemble the ideal bed. Indeed, it is their resemblance to the ideal bed which entitles beds in the sensible world to be classified as beds. Another way of explicating the theory is to say that sensible objects are the mirror images of the ideal forms. The Platonist is sometimes said to regard the sensible world as an extremely smoky mirror; and those who "look in the mirror" are treated to badly blurred images of the ideal forms. Further explication of the Theory of Ideas requires an answer to the question, "What difficulties is a use of the theory expected to resolve?"

There is a family of difficulties which the Theory of Ideas

might be expected to resolve. First of all, for some philosophers the world of sense does not provide satisfactory objects of knowledge; and Ideas are an alternative more to their taste. The Platonist's complaint against the world of sense may be stated in this way. Animals and plants, stars and rocks, tables and tablets, nature and all man's artifacts are subject to change. The world of sense is a world of growth and decay, waxing and waning, multiplication and disintegration, time and passage. The world of sense is a world of impermanence. Since it is always subject to change, no knowledge of this world can be certain; and indeed for those philosophers who desire permanent, eternal objects of knowledge, the world of sense appears to be absolutely unknowable. But there is some cheer in the prospect of studying not animals but the Idea or Form of which all animals partake—animalness. Thus animalness, and similarly, plantness, starness, rockness, tableness, tabletness, and other essences are discovered to be the eternal and unchanging objects of knowledge. Plato is thought by some philosophers to have made use of the Theory of Ideas in the way I have just described as a means of escaping Heraclitus' conclusion that everything is in flux. There are some things that are not in flux—Ideas. Thus, there are some things that can be known—Ideas. So the claim that knowledge is impossible, since all there is to know is the unknowable sensible world, is refuted.

A second difficulty which the Theory of Ideas is expected to resolve is the puzzle over how general words have meaning. Any word in the dictionary, except proper names and exclamations, is a general word. The puzzle about their meaning may be stated in this way: How do I know when to say that something is white? It must be that I have an idea of whiteness, a picture in my head, which I may look at with my "inner eye." Then, whenever I wonder whether the snow or my tablecloth or my hair is white, I compare the color of the object with my idea of whiteness, and if they match, I may call the object white. My own idea of whiteness is my knowledge of the Idea of White; and, the argument declares, if there were no objective Idea of White against which we might measure our particular judgments of white snow and white tablecloths and white hair, how could we ever be sure that anything is really white? Similarly there must be Ideas of all general words. If there were not such Ideas, how could I be sure that anything I see is really what I believe it to be?

A third difficulty which the Theory of Ideas is expected to resolve is a special case of those already mentioned. It is the puzzle of how value words, particularly moral words, have meaning. "Nice," "pretty," "swell," "fine," "o.k.," "delightful," and "interesting" are examples of value words. Moral words are a special class of value words. Plato was especially interested in the moral words "just," "good," and "virtuous" and others like them; and I think that a good case could be made for saying that Plato thought that the Theory of Ideas was most valuable in explaining the meaning of moral words. His estimate of its value depended in part on his respect for geometry. Geometers were of special interest to Plato because the practice of their science requires them to think in abstractions. Their propositions are about *the* circle and *the* right triangle. Their diagrams are but representations of ideal lines and angles. Their proofs prove not just the drawn case but all like cases for all time. Now, geometers would be especially able to appreciate Plato's view of the meaning of moral words. For he thought that when someone said that a certain man was a just man or that a certain deed was a good deed, the words "just" and "good" took their meanings from the Idea of Justice and the Idea of the Good. Just as geometers' talk about the drawn figure is really talk about that figure in the abstract, so Plato thought that talk about justice and goodness should be understood as talk about the Idea of Justice and the Idea of the Good. Indeed, he argued, how could we ever be sure that any man is just, if we do not perceive in him some resemblance to the Idea of Justice? How could we ever be sure that some deed is a good deed, if we do not perceive in it some resemblance to the Idea of the Good. These words "just" and "good" and others like them must be the names of abstract, objective qualities, or else, it is claimed, we could never make any meaningful moral statements; and we could never have any knowledge of good and bad.

The difficulties which the Theory of Ideas is intended to resolve may be resolved without supposing that anything like the Theory of Ideas is true; and I shall now consider each of them in turn.

Any account of how general words come to be meaningful must be prefaced by the remark that there are different kinds of general words—nouns, adjectives, and verbs, for example. So it is only fair to warn the reader that no one explanation may account for the meaningfulness of all kinds of general words. Granting this preface, I shall offer no more than one answer to the question of how general words have meaning; but it is an answer designed to free us from any need to use the Theory of Ideas to account for the meaning of general words.

The Platonist account of meaning which I wish to dispose of is that general words work like proper names. The word "white" is claimed to be the name of the Idea of White. "White" means the Idea of White. This account of meaning may be objected to on the ground that it does not do justice to the way in which we learn to use general words. The theory implies that a child could never learn to use "white" until he had learned to recognize the Idea of White. But in teaching a child to use the word "white" nothing is ever said about the Idea of White; rather, a child is shown a glass of milk or the new-fallen snow or a fresh crib sheet and taught to call these things "white." He soon catches the notion that those things which resemble the examples in color may also be called "white." Some very logical children may practice calling everything that is non-white, "not white," for a while, just to make sure that they have caught the hang of the concept "white." Notice that there is a sense in which one never finishes learning how to use a general word. For in each fresh case in which it might be used, one has to decide whether it is again applicable. The meanings of general words have hazy edges. To return to "white," one has to learn when white slides into off-white and then into light gray. Or again, where does white leave off and ivory or cream begin? Knowing the meaning of general words, then, is knowing the range of their applicability: when they can and when they cannot be used. The criterion of use is roughly one of consistency with past usage, and not only past usage of the particular general word in question, but with that of the whole family to which it belongs, and even the families to which it is opposed. "White" also owes something to "black."

It may be asked whether this account of how general words come to have meaning is a refutation of the Theory of Ideas. No, it is not. What I have tried to do here is show that the Theory of Ideas need not be invoked to resolve the problem of how general words have meaning. There is one less philosophical problem which requires its use.

The problem of accounting for the meaning of moral words is to be resolved along lines similar to those followed in accounting for the meaning of general words. A child learns from his parents how to use moral words, just as he learns how to use other families of words, such as color words, object words, and verbs. First he uses "good" and "bad" as his parents do; and then he extends his use of these words in new situations as their resemblance to old, familiar situations warrants. The justification for the way in which he uses these words is not that he has apprehended the Idea of the Good, but that he uses these words in ways that are consistent with his parents' use of them. And what justifies the parents' use of these words? They in turn might appeal to the practice of their parents; but ultimately someone must be found who can show that moral words are used as they are in moral judgments because the making and observing of these moral judgments implements a certain ideal of social harmony. What is required then to assure us that moral words are meaningful is not the existence of Ideas but the explication of the ideal of social harmony which illuminates the context in which these moral words are used.

The question of whether Ideas are the only satisfactory objects of knowledge turns largely on what is meant by "satisfactory." Here I wish to consider the Theory of Ideas on its merits, quite apart from any reasons for its psychological attractiveness to certain philosophers. From this point of view, there is much that can be said about why Ideas are not satisfactory objects of knowledge. Critics of Ideas may be divided into two sorts. Either they question the existence of Ideas, or they argue that assuming their existence raises insoluble problems.

The question of whether or not Ideas exist, or to put it more delicately, "How do we know Ideas?" is extremely difficult to answer. Their most famous partisan, Plato, was exceedingly vague about how one comes to know Ideas. Indeed, in his dialogue *Parmenides,* he presents the argument that no one can ever know Ideas, for, since their nature and ours are absolutely different, they must forever remain incomprehensible to us. But supposing that you can attempt to know Ideas, Plato offers directions for trying that go something like this: In the first place, not everyone ought to try. But if you do, you ought not to try until you are in your fifties, have led an orderly and moderate life with plenty of physical exercise, and have an advanced taste for music and geometry. From there you are on your own. The difficulty of knowing Ideas is nicely illustrated in this report of an exchange between Plato and Diogenes the Cynic:

> When Plato was discoursing about his "ideas," and using the nouns "tableness" and "cupness"; "I, O Plato!" interrupted Diogenes, "see a table and a cup, but I see no tableness or cupness." Plato made answer, "That is natural enough, for you have eyes, by which a cup and a table are contemplated; but you have not intellect, by which tableness and cupness are seen." [1]

Unfortunately Plato leaves the matter at this point. If you can know Ideas, they exist. But you are not entitled to infer their non-existence from your inability to know them. But this state of affairs should make us suspicious of Plato's rejoinder "you have not intellect." Diogenes' deficiency would seem to be not intellect but interest in the kind of philosophical problems that bothered Plato. If no evidence is relevant to establishing the non-existence of Ideas, questioning their existence is unfruitful. The proper line of questioning is this: How useful are Ideas in the resolution of philosophical problems?

It may be argued that not only does the Theory of Ideas resolve no philosophical problems, it generates more entities than a phil-

[1] *The Lives and Opinions of Eminent Philosophers* by Diogenes Laertius, translated by C. D. Yonge (London, G. Bell & Sons), 1895, p. 236.

osopher knows what to do with. Consider the plight of someone who wants to learn something about the world, and who is told that he must make use of the Theory of Ideas. He is told, for example, that he can identify men as men because they resemble the Idea of Man. "But," the puzzled philosopher may ask, "what guarantees the resemblance of men to the Idea of Man?" If the Theory of Ideas is consistently applied, the answer must be that both men and the Idea of Man resemble yet another Idea, the Idea of the Idea of Man. Then, of course, the resemblance of both men and the Idea of Man to this second Idea is guaranteed by yet another Idea. The hierarchy of guarantees requires more and more Ideas, until the mind is staggered by the prospect. Curiously enough, Plato himself was familiar with this criticism of the Theory of Ideas, and even stated it in the *Parmenides*. Since this dialogue is thought to be one of Plato's late works, and since it contains no answer to the criticism, some philosophers have thought that these considerations taken together show that Plato was by no means eternally wedded to the Theory of Ideas.

Plato's great pupil Aristotle objects to the Theory of Ideas, because it is of no use in solving the problem of causation. It is all very well to say that certain objects are chairs because they resemble the Idea of Chairness. But how did these several pieces of wood joined together in the chair before me come to be a chair? This is a kind of question which cannot be answered by an appeal to an Idea, for it is not in the nature of an Idea to make anything. The Theory of Ideas is useless to Aristotle for it throws no light on the problem of the efficient cause of the world. Indeed, the theory enlarges the problem in an alarming way. For we need to ask the additional question, "What caused the Ideas?"

For these and other reasons which Aristotle and other critics of the theory advance, Ideas seem not to be satisfactory objects of knowledge. The last hope for those who seek eternal and immutable objects of knowledge is the concepts of mathematics. These are certainly eternal and immutable, and thus thoroughly satisfactory, so long as one can be content with objects of knowledge

that exist only in the mind. Many a partisan of the Theory of
Ideas, however, has hoped that he was learning about a part of
the world, or better, the only real world. Yet I have tried gently
to relieve him of this hope. If he is to learn about the world, he
must travel with us into the realm of empirical knowledge. But
before we come to that topic, I must carry the reader through
yet another philosophical extravagance.

## THE IDEALIST'S WORLD

I now want to consider the view that the stuff of the world is
ideas. Philosophers who hold this opinion are called Idealists; and
their view of the world is stated negatively as the claim that
matter does not exist. As the reader may have guessed, an exposition of Idealism requires a new definition of "idea." There is a
difference between seeing a circus and thinking about a circus
one has seen; and these "thinking about" cases are cases which
we would ordinarily describe by saying that someone is having
ideas. The Idealist does use "idea" in this way; but at the same
time he also wants to use the word in a way peculiar to himself.
He wants to use it to mean "sensation," and, more peculiar still,
he wants to use "idea" in place of "material object." But even as
he uses the word in these new ways, he wants it to keep the color
it has in our usual distinction between seeing something and
thinking of it.

How does the Idealist use "idea" to mean "sensation"? He
wants to say that when he sees the circus he is having ideas of
the circus. What he is saying is that when he sees the aerialist
dangling from a flying trapeze, he is having aerialist and trapeze
images on the retinas of his eyes. When he hears the band play
"The Stars and Stripes Forever," he is having march music
sensations on his ear drums. When he smells the elephants, he
is having elephant-smell sensations on the tips of his olfactory
nerves. When the spun sugar candy melts on his tongue, he is
having spun-sugar-candy sensations on the taste buds of his
tongue. Finally, as his backside tires on the hard bleacher seats,
he is having bleacher-seat feelings through the seat of his pants.

The curious thing here is talking about retina images; about the stimulation of ear drums, olfactory nerves, and taste buds; and about sensations of touch as ideas. This use of "idea" was introduced by Locke, who spoke of "ideas of sensation," and it has stuck in philosophy as a piece of professional jargon. But it is not only confusing, it is downright misleading; and while its misleading character at first makes Idealism appear to be possible, in the end it makes it untenable.

Let us go to the circus again. From our bleacher seats we watch the man on the flying trapeze, and I say, "I see the man on the flying trapeze." Now this is a thoroughly ordinary thing for me to say; and my saying it will hardly startle you. What if I say, "I am having man-on-the-flying-trapeze images on the retinas of my eyes"? This statement, too, is not startling, although translating my first statement into the language of ophthalmology does seem a roundabout way of talking about seeing. But now suppose that I say, "I see man-on-the-flying-trapeze images on the retinas of my eyes." This statement is startling, for you know that no one can see his own eyes (remember that when I look in a mirror, I am only seeing *mirror images* of my eyes), let alone his retinas and images on those retinas. Indeed, my saying that I *have* images on the retinas of my eyes, when I see, depends either on my supposing that the principles of ophthalmology are applicable to my eyes, or my taking my ophthalmologist's word for it after he has examined my eyes. But we must keep straight what I can say and what an ophthalmologist can say. I can never talk about my own eyes as though I were an ophthalmologist examining them. I can only say, "I see the man on the flying trapeze." Unless we have included an ophthalmologist complete with ophthalmoscope in our circus party, no one can say, "I see the images on the retinas"; and even then the ophthalmologist is not talking about his own eyes.

Now it is a mixing up of what I can say about my seeing and what an ophthalmologist can say about it that leads to Idealism. For the Idealist supposes that I can talk about my seeing in the way that an ophthalmologist can, so that whenever I can say, "I see the apple," I can say, "I see apple images on the retinas of my eyes." Or to use the general term "idea," I can say, "I see apple ideas." Indeed, it is at this point that the Idealist takes the definitive step and says that all I *really* can say is, "I see apple ideas." For, supposing that I must talk about my seeing in the way an ophthalmologist can, the Idealist claims that all I can see is apple images on the retinas of my eyes. Similarly I must speak of smelling, hearing, tasting, and touching as though the object of these operations were my sensations and not elephants, music, spun sugar candy, and bleacher seats. Thus, according to the Idealist, I can know nothing but ideas. Indeed, says the Idealist, since I can only claim existence for what I know, and ideas are the only things known by me, it must be that the world is nothing but ideas—mental clean through. But I trust that I have already made it clear that the issue is not what the world is made of, but how I perceive the world and consequently what I may say of the world. Since we do not perceive sensations as the Idealist claims we do, we have no good reason for saying as he does that the world is nothing but ideas.

What we do learn from Idealism is not that the world is nothing but ideas, but that our *knowledge* of the world is nothing but our "ideas." It is not true that the circus is nothing but ideas. But it is true that my knowledge of the circus amounts to my having seen certain sights and smelled certain smells and heard certain sounds, and so on. Now, allowing that there need be no discussion, here, about whether or not a line may be drawn between where my perceptions leave off and the world begins, I may speak of the difference between my seeing and what I see, between my smelling and what I smell, between my hearing and what I hear, and so on. Then it follows that if all I know about certain sights is what I see, I can claim that what I can see exists, only when I am seeing it. Similarly, if all I know about certain sounds is what I hear, I can claim that what I hear exists, only when I am hearing it. And the same sort of thing must be said of whatever I can learn about by using my other senses. The point, then, of general interest which Idealists make when they say that the world is nothing but ideas is that we have no grounds for claiming that something exists when we are not perceiving it.

But why should the Idealist want to say that the world is nothing but ideas? He does so for the best of philosophical reasons. He has discovered a fault in a philosophical view of the world, and he is trying to construct a replacement. The philosophical view and its fault may be described in this way. As I have already noted in the previous section, some philosophers find change to be a distressing aspect of the world. Everything that is part of the physical world grows older, and most things change in many other ways too. With all of this change going on around us, how can we say that anything we perceive now is the same thing that we perceived at an earlier time? Or how can we say that anything we perceive now will be the same thing that we shall perceive in the future? One of the notable answers to these questions is the claim that "behind" or "beneath" any object that we perceive there lies an imperceptible substance or prime matter that supports the object that we perceive. Indeed the object that we do perceive is but a collection of qualities that are held together by the object's unseen substance. It is only at the superficial level of these qualities that change takes place. Beneath them lies the unchanged and unchanging substance; and the supposition of its existence provides the uneasy philosopher with the permanence he requires perceptible objects to have.

The story works until the Idealist is troubled by a new kind of uneasiness. If we cannot perceive this substance, how do we know that it exists? With this question the suppositional character of substance is exposed. Perhaps it was a good and useful supposition; but alas it must be admitted that it is no more than a supposition. Hence, the Idealist's denial of substance or matter. But this denial must not be understood as the denial of the existence of anything that we ordinarily claim exists because we perceive it. What the Idealist does deny is that any of these things is a "material object," that is, something that might exist unperceived because it is supported by substance or philosopher's matter. For the Idealist, shoes and ships and sealing wax are not material objects but "ideas," that is, things dependent for their existence on a perceiving mind.

But while the Idealist has shown the assumption of substance to be unwarranted, the problem of change remains, and is even complicated by the Idealist's claim that being perceived is the criterion of existence. Idealists have felt that some explanation must be offered for the regularity of the world's character. I do find my tea cups in my china cupboard, even though I have not been watching them since I last washed them and put them away. It does seem to be too extreme to say that the world goes out of existence each time I shut my eyes and comes into existence again each time I open them. So the position which many Idealists take is that since the world is nothing but ideas, we may very well regard the world as God's mind. Then the explanation of my regularly perceiving certain things is that God thinks of them all the time. This view of the world has made it a cozy place for many an otherwise homeless Idealist. But alas, there is a glaring difficulty in this view. For if the only evidence I have for my tea cup's existence is that I now perceive it, am I not making an unwarranted assumption when I claim that God exists, just because I think I hold in my hand the same tea cup which I held yesterday? After all, I perceive only my tea cup and not God. On the Idealist's own grounds, God is a no more likely explanation of the preservation and continuation of what we see than substance was. Whether there can be good grounds for saying that something exists when I am not perceiving it, is a question to be pursued in the next section.

The view that all we know of the world is what we perceive is one which Idealists share with empiricists. Now that we have rejected the Idealist claim that the world is nothing but ideas, it remains for us to see what empiricists make of the world as experience.

## THE EMPIRICIST'S WORLD

The heart of empiricism is the empirical criterion of existence. To convince an empiricist that what you are talking about does, or might, exist, you must convince him that he, and other people besides yourself, can or might experience it. If your statements about what there is are to be meaningful to an empiricist, he must know how he might go about discovering the existence or non-existence of what you are talking about.

Suppose that you are helping me lay the table for tea, and I say to you, "The tea cups are on the top shelf of the china closet." This is a statement of existence, for I am claiming that there are tea cups, and that they are in a certain place. For you to understand this statement, you must know how I am using it. If you do not know, you could not begin to judge my claim that the tea cups exist. But if you know, you can look for and find my china closet. (My making the statement implies that I am talking about my china closet. At least on first hearing, you would not take me to be implying, in an extremely oblique way, that you should steal some cups from my neighbor's china closet.) Having found my china closet and its top shelf, and knowing what a tea cup is, you can see for yourself that the tea cups are or are not where I claimed them to be. The touchstone of your understanding the statement is your knowing how I am using it. This condition deserves a word. If I use the phrase "tea cup" in the way in which you use the phrase "sherry glass," when you find sherry glasses on the top shelf of my china closet, you may believe that you have discovered that there are no tea cups there. But what you have really discovered is that we were not talking about the same thing. It is well to be alert to the possibility of this kind of conclusion to many disputes about existence.

Something must also be said about what the empiricist means by "experience." At the very least he means your use of your five senses: sight, hearing, taste, touch, and smell. But few empiricists would want to limit their claims of existence to what can be perceived by the unaided senses. The extension of sight, for example, by means of microscopes, telescopes, and fluoroscopes is not only allowed but welcomed. What is more, most empiricists would want to allow indirect evidence of existence. For example, the use of photographic plates to record events which occur too quickly to be seen by the human eye, or the use of a pointer mov-

ing across a dial or a stylus arm marking on a graph paper to
record events which, even though invisible to the human eye,
may activate pointers or stylus arms, as happenings in the interior
of an atom smasher may be made to do.

There is yet another qualification of experience which empiricists make and which must be enlarged upon. For me to claim
that I have learned something by experience, my experience must
be one that others can have. Indeed, if they cannot have the same
kind of experience, how can they understand what I am talking
about? For me to be able to claim that there is a horse in the
quad right now, other people must be able to see the horse.
Seeing is an empirically acceptable way of finding out about
horses. Lassoing them, feeding them carrots and sugar, and pat-
ting their noses are other empirical ways of finding out about
horses. When I say, "There's a horse in the quad," and you look
(look carefully) and find none, you are entitled to say, "You're
wrong. There isn't any horse in the quad." When I say, "Oh, you
misunderstood me. I was referring to that horselike bush over
there," you may certainly reply, "Well, do say what you mean!"
What you look for depends on your understanding of the directions which you are given.

If I say to you, "I've just seen a squg in the garden," as an
empiricist your first move would be to ask, "What's a squg?" If
I tell you that a squg is a kind of snail, and you know what snails
are, you will know what to look for if you want to try to see
a squg. But what if I tell you that neither you nor anyone else
can see or touch or hear or stumble over squgs? I am the only
person who can know the squgs in the garden. As an empiricist,
the mildest thing you can say to me is, "Well, I know that you
are claiming that there are squgs in the garden, but your word
is no guarantee of their existence. I might take your word, if there
were, at least in principle, a way of my checking it. But if no
one but you can know squgs, then no check is possible. Here there
is no guarantee against your making a fool out of me."

I now want to characterize the empiricist's world a little more
fully. I hope I have made it clear that, whatever else it is, it is
a world of observables. To qualify as a part of the world, what-

ever is being talked about must in some way be the sort of thing that can be experienced; and the way in which it can be experienced classifies its status in the world. I can both see and handle my tea cup, and being able to do these things leads me to classify it as a material object. But the limits of the phrase "material object" are nicely illustrated by the question, "Is a rainbow a material object?" It can certainly be seen; but precise people may feel that we press language too far when we claim that by touching the water droplets whose refraction and reflection of sunlight make the rainbow, we are touching the rainbow. It would seem, then, that we must allow that along with material objects our world contains visual phenomena like rainbows; and we must also count in sounds, smells, tastes, and tactile qualities. What is more, relations such as "north of," "father of," "friend of," "blacker than," and "The baby weighs 7 pounds," to name only a few examples, also have a place in the world.

Is there any place at which the empiricist will draw a line between what exists and what does not exist? First of all, he insists that there are differences in existential status depending on the kind of experience relevant to knowing about something. The empiricist would regard a person as violating this principle if he talked about the number one in the same way that he talked about his tea cup, expecting to find it laid up in a numerical closet, wondering how old it is, and so on. Tea cups and the number one just do not fit into experience in the same way. Similarly, friendship, electromagnetism, the cost-of-living index, comic strip characters, and tea cups have different statuses in the world. Each of these things is to be looked for in a different way. Now whether there is anything in the world whose existence an empiricist will flatly deny depends on whether its description contains a self-contradiction. For example, an empiricist would feel justified in denying the existence of ghosts, so long as they are described as having incorporeal bodies, that is, bodies that are not bodies. For the contradictory character of the phrase "incorporeal body" makes it absolutely useless as a direction for finding a ghost. Contrast this talk about ghosts with someone's telling an empiricist that there is a lavender elephant outside his

study door. Now there is nothing self-contradictory about the
phrase "lavender elephant." One does not expect to see one; but
there is nothing impossible about there being one, especially if
one has playful friends who might paint up an elephant and
bring it around just to make a point. So the empiricist cannot
flatly deny (or for that matter immediately affirm) the existence
of the lavender elephant. He must first take a look. Here, in
contrast with ghosts, we have a case in which experience is the
criterion of existence.

What the empiricist is looking for as the basis of our knowledge of the world is regularity in both qualities and behavior.
For it is on the basis of regularity that he identifies individuals and
that he has expectations about the causal properties of anything.
To complete this sketch of the empiricist's world, I must discuss
these uses of regularity.

How does the empiricist deal with the problem of individuation
or sameness? His empiricism contains this difficulty: If all I
know of my tea cup is gained by experience, how do I know that
today's tea cup is the same tea cup I used yesterday? I think it is.
But what grounds do I have for thinking so? It seems that I might
have good grounds for saying so, if I had kept watch on it from
tea time yesterday to tea time today. I should have to keep awake
for twenty-four hours, of course, and be careful not to let my
gaze wander. Obviously I could not trust someone else to watch
for me, for then I should have to keep watch on him to make
sure that he is the same watcher I had posted in the beginning.
But even if I did stay awake watching my cup for twenty-four
hours, I should be sure of the sameness of my tea cup for only a
comparatively short period of time. At this point the empiricist
may very well break in to say, "Really, what has been said so
far is a travesty of empiricism's account of how you know that the
tea cup you are using today is the same cup you used yesterday.
The proper question to start with is, 'How could you tell that
it is *not* the same cup?'" Shall we start again?

In the first place, my tea cup is the only one of its kind that
I own. (If I owned more than one in the same pattern, it might be
difficult, though not in principle impossible, to tell them apart.)

I remember that I put my cup in the china closet when I washed up after tea yesterday. Now, at tea time today, I take it down, all ready for my Lapsang Souchong liquor. But wait, is this the *same* tea cup I put away yesterday? Well, it looks the same. No unexplained chips. No hitherto unnoticed eccentricities in the flower pattern, which I have studied for innumerable tea times. The weight is right. The "clink" is right. I can devise no test which might show me that it is a different cup. No irregularity is detectable. Then why not say that it is the same cup? Doubts about someone's stealing in and substituting another cup, and my never being able to tell the difference, are unreal doubts. Unreal, because they could in principle never be resolved. I know how to resolve real doubts. If I think that Mrs. Jenkins got our tea cups mixed up, when she brought hers over for tea yesterday, we can compare our cups in the hope of finding a difference that will help me decide whether a mix-up has occurred. ("Notice," says Mrs. J., "the roses on your cup never were as pink as mine.") If I can find no difference, no irregularities, my unfounded doubts about sameness must be dismissed. To engage in irresolvable doubts is quite properly called "philosopher's doubt." Only philosophers, including small children, can find the time for it.

What does the empiricist say of our knowledge of causation? If we are to continue living, we desperately need to know what causes what. How did I burn my finger? How did the tea get in my cup? What happened to my collar button? How do you get from Russellville, Arkansas, to Minneapolis, Minnesota? What will serve as a filament for an electric light? These, and millions of questions like them, are causal questions; and what the empiricist claims to have done is to provide an analysis of the knowledge which enables us to answer them.

The empiricist analyzes our knowledge of causation into a knowledge of regularities. Life requires that I know more than that the orange I am now eating is edible, or at the very least is not immediately poisonous. What I should like to know is that all oranges are edible. Or, to ask only for what is possible in the empiricist's world, I must be able to suppose that all oranges are edible. What good reasons can I have for doing so? Only experience can provide them. Until I try my first orange, I can presume to know nothing about its edibility, even though I may be inclined to take the word of others. But after my first orange, I may have certain expectations about all oranges. In so far as future oranges resemble the orange I ate in immediately observable characteristics, it is my belief that they will resemble it in untried characteristics, i.e. that they too are tasty and digestible. From resemblance in one respect I feel entitled to expect resemblance in another; and the oftener I experience a regular connection between the look of an orange and its edibility, the greater are my expectations of finding this connection in the next orange I eat.

The promise and the risk in this kind of thinking are obvious. Everything turns on the care with which one judges the immediate similarities between the orange one has and the oranges one has known, before supposing their regular connection with possible similarities. Even when care is taken, the empiricist makes no promise of certainty, for one of the tenets of empiricism is that it is conceivable that the world might have changed since one learned about some causal connection. Indeed, were it not logically possible for one's causal expectations to go unfulfilled, they would not be empirical knowledge. The empiricist claims no knowledge of causal connections outside of experience, and since he has not yet had experience of the future, and of necessity cannot have it, his experience will not justify hope for unfailing causal connections. Causal expectations are always in doubt until they have been tested.

For the empiricist, a knowledge of nature is a knowledge of the regular way in which things behave. Thus, in its empirical aspect, natural science is a collection of generalizations, called "natural laws," which summarize the past and point to the future. They describe the way in which things have happened in the past, and predict the way things will happen in the future. The empiricist's grand philosophical assumption is that nature is orderly, and both the scientist and the common man assent to this principle in practice.

I must not, however, leave the reader with the impression that the natural scientist's task, closely connected as it is with empiricism, is merely collecting the regularities which are to be found in nature. One of the equally important ways in which the natural scientist spends his time is in thinking up regularities to collect. For example, John Dalton (1766-1844) is counted as one of the founders of modern chemistry because he thought up a way of conceiving atoms so that they might be looked for. His suggestion was that atoms be regarded as having different weights, thus opening the way to distinguishing different kinds of atoms. Since chemists knew how to carry out the operation of weighing, Dalton's dictum, "Atoms have weight," was of interest and importance to them, for it suggested a way in which atoms, if they existed, might be brought within the range of chemists' experience. Because his speculation was fruitful, Dalton is a hero of science. Not all such speculations are as fruitful, but this does not mean that speculation is to be discouraged. For there is no way of telling beforehand when it will pay off. But what I want to stress here is that atoms did not come knocking at Dalton's door and say, "Look at us! We are part of the world too." Dalton had to think of a way of going out and finding atoms. That they could be found is one of the glories of the empirical side of natural science; but that the empirical side is heavily dependent on the speculative side must never be forgotten.

## PHILOSOPHY AND WORLD VIEWS

We have now examined the world views of the Platonist, the Idealist, and the empiricist. These views are very different. In the Platonist's world, a realm of Ideas stands brightly over a shadowy world of sense ready to enthrall minds exalted enough to apprehend it. In the Idealist's world, all objects are mental, even those which we would ordinarily call material. In the empiricist's world, a firm line is drawn between what can be thought of and what can be experienced, and only the latter may be counted as existing. Although these world views are three of the most famous, they are but a tiny fraction of the total number of world views which philosophers have invented.

Why have philosophers thought up these disparate world views? Why, for example, cannot a Platonist and an empiricist agree that Ideas exist? Notice what agreement would require. For the empiricist to agree that Ideas might be known, he would have to become a Platonist. For the Platonist to agree that Ideas need not be known, he would have to become an empiricist. Our question then takes a new form: Why do neither empiricists become Platonists, nor Platonists become empiricists? The short answer is that neither is interested in solving the sort of problem which the adoption of the other's world view permits one to solve. Indeed, for each one the other's philosophical problems are non-existent. No empiricist tries to find an answer to the question of how one apprehends Ideas, for by definition they are not the sort of thing which he expects to experience. No Platonist tries to find an answer to the question of whether today's tea cup is the same tea cup he drank from yesterday, for by definition the life history of a mere tea cup is beneath his professional notice. But why are philosophers interested in problems so different that they force the invention of different, even incompatible, world views?

I have said that philosophers try to understand the world as a whole; but there appear to be two fundamentally divergent views of how the world is to be understood. On the one hand there are those philosophers who believe that in itself the world is incomprehensible and that the philosopher must search out some extraordinary state of affairs that lies concealed behind or beyond the surface of the world. When, and only when, it is discovered, the world itself will become understandable. On the other hand, there are those philosophers who believe that the world is understandable in and of itself, and that what is required is not the pursuit of the extraordinary but the careful analysis of the ordinary. The first of these conceptions of philosophy is illustrated by both Platonism and Idealism; and the second, by empiricism.

In both Platonism and Idealism the philosopher is expected to be able to gain some special knowledge which is only available to philosophers, and which consequently only he is able to publish to the rest of mankind. In Platonism, it is the philosopher who learns about Ideas and reports their significance to mankind. In Idealism, it is the philosopher who sees the mental character of the world and who teaches mankind to avoid misapprehensions about matter. In contrast with these views of the philosopher's role, consider the task which he is given in empiricism. He is not asked to discover either some realm above the world or some mysterious aspect of the world. He is only expected to make clear beliefs which everyone has about the world (that this tea cup is the same one I used yesterday, that oranges are nourishing), and to show in what respects these beliefs are justified. He reveals nothing mysterious or hidden. Rather he tells us what anyone could have figured out, if he had only stopped to think—like a philosopher.

The little bit more which I can add is to notice that those philosophers who engage in the pursuit of the extraordinary have very often turned to philosophy as a kind of substitute for religion. They expect to find by philosophical methods what religion promises to give only by revelation. But the curious thing about the great body of thought and literature called philosophy is that those philosophers who undertake to explicate the ordinary also expect to accomplish their task by philosophical method. It is method, then, which gives philosophy its unity, but not peace. For each kind of philosopher feels free to turn philosophical method against the other to show either that he is mistaken in his conception of the philosophical enterprise, or in his employment of philosophical method, or in his philosophical conclusions. To the reader I recommend a task requiring patience and thoroughness. It is the examination of each piece of philosophy on its own merits.

### SUGGESTIONS FOR FURTHER READING

Along with Plato's *Republic* one should look at his criticism of Ideas or Forms in the first part of the *Parmenides*. Aristotle's criticism of Ideas occurs in the *Metaphysics,* Bk. I, Ch. 9, and in the *Nicomachean Ethics,* Bk. I, Ch. 6.

Berkeley's *Three Dialogues Between Hylas and Philonous* is an extension and defense of the Idealist views expressed in his *Principles of Human Knowledge. The Spirit of Modern Philosophy* by Josiah Royce (Braziller, New York, 1955) is a refined statement of Idealism by a recent American philosopher.

The original statement of Hume's empiricism is his *Treatise of Human Nature* (Oxford University Press, New York, 1941). *An Inquiry Concerning Human Understanding* is a streamlined version of Book I of the *Treatise.* The historically minded reader may care to trace empiricism backward to the *Essay Concerning Human Understanding* by John Locke, a book which influenced both Berkeley and Hume. Locke's own views were formed as a criticism of René Descartes's theory of knowledge. Descartes's principal philosophical works are the *Discourse on Method* and the *Meditations.*

Two modern extensions of empiricism are Pragmatism and Logical Positivism. For an introduction to the former one may read *Pragmatism* by William James (Meridian). A much shorter statement of Pragmatism is Charles S. Peirce's essay "How To Make Our Ideas Clear" which may be found in any one of several collections of Peirce's writing. The most exciting statement of the logical positivists' point of view is *Language, Truth and Logic* by A. J. Ayer (Dover).

## FOUR

The following items are suggested for joint reading with this chapter: *Summa Theologica* by St. Thomas Aquinas, First Part, Question 1, "The Nature and Extent of Sacred Doctrine," and Question 2, "The Existence of God" (*Summa Theologica,* Vol. I, Benziger, New York, 1947); *Dialogues Concerning Natural Religion* by David Hume; *An Inquiry Concerning Human Understanding* by David Hume, Chapter X, "Of Miracles."

# Philosophy and God

Philosophical method has often been used in attempts to prove that God exists, and in this chapter I want to examine and criticize some of these attempts. But before we look at arguments to prove God's existence, something must be said about why Christians have taken an interest in providing a philosophical answer to the question "Does God exist?" A discussion of this Christian interest will illustrate to some extent a problem of communication which is also inherent in the other two great monotheistic religions, Judaism and Islam.

Christians are interested in the question "Does God exist?" because of a task which has been imposed on them by their founder. He said to them, "Go ye therefore and teach all nations. . . ." (Matthew 24:19) Hence, Christians are bound to try to convert all people to Christianity. But they labor under difficulties illustrated by the following dialogue between a Christian and a non-Christian:

*Christian:* By listening to someone who preaches from the Bible or by reading the Bible yourself, you can find out what God expects of you.

*Non-Christian:* But why should I be interested in the Bible?

*Christian:* It is a record of the word of God.

*Non-Christian:* How do you know that?

*Christian:* It says in the Bible again and again that the word of God is being reported.

*Non-Christian:* But aren't you arguing in a circle? The word of God is in the Bible because the Bible says that it is the word of God. This is not a very happy proof. Can you prove independently of the Bible that it is the word of God? What would you say if I denied that it is?

*Christian:* Well, I can only say that for centuries people have accepted it as such. You'll just have to take their word for it that the Bible is the word of God.

*Non-Christian:* But since the original people who accepted the Bible as the word of God are beyond recall, we have no way of finding out whether they had good reasons for doing so. This last argument, then, is not a very good one either. Therefore I still cannot accept the Bible as the word of God.

*Christian:* But you are missing Christianity.

*Non-Christian:* From the very dubious arguments you use to interest me in it, it appears to be no loss to me.

*Christian:* (To himself in despair) But *you* are lost to Christianity. I am failing as a missionary. How can I convince argumentative non-Christians that they should become Christians?

The Christian missionary's problem is to find common ground with the non-Christian, or else no discussion of Christianity can ever begin. Obviously the Bible cannot provide this common ground, because the non-Christian does not respect it as a source of religious teaching. If he did, he would be a Christian. St. Thomas Aquinas's solution of the missionary's problem of common ground is human reason, by which he means our ability to follow arguments. Both Christians and non-Christians are capable of following arguments; and the Christian's task is to provide arguments for non-Christians that will lead them to a knowledge of God, from whence they may be led into Christianity. I cannot forbear remarking that the task of identifying a god whose nature may be rationally established with the revealed god of Christianity must be a formidable one. Presumably the Christian adherence to monotheism provides the required premise: If a god's existence can be proved, since Christians believe that only one god exists, the god whose existence has been proved must be the Christian god. But the labor of identifying the philosopher's god with the god of Christian revelation need trouble us only if philosophy succeeds in proving God's existence. Aquinas himself was supremely confident of the power of philosophy. Using the philosopher's tools of careful definitions and premises that cannot be denied, he endeavored to supply missionaries with an arsenal of arguments that would be helpful in their meetings with non-Christians, particularly arguments proving God's existence. His work is worthy of our attention, for it is still esteemed by many people who believe that God's existence may be proved by philosophical argument.

## PROVING GOD'S EXISTENCE

The Christian philosopher who attempts to prove God's existence must work within the limits of the Christian conception of God's nature. God is thought of as being apart from the world; and thus he is said to be "immaterial," a word which is used to show that God is unlike anything in the world in form, though not in function. That is, God may be said to be a father; but this only means that he cares for his worshipers as a father cares for his children, and not that he has the bodily form of a human father. Even though God is thought to be apart from the world, he is nonetheless thought to be the creator of the world and still capable of effecting changes in it.

At first glance, the philosopher's task looks impossible. He must prove to human beings in the world the existence of a supramundane being; and the descriptions of their respective natures as "material" and "immaterial" appear to imply a self-contradiction in the suggestion that men might know God. Aquinas attempts to overcome this difficulty through distinguishing two different kinds of knowledge of existence, direct and indirect. Anyone to whom God revealed himself (allowing God the power of overcoming the gap between the material and the immaterial) would have a direct knowledge of God. When I have indirect knowledge of existence, I infer the existence of B from the existence of A, whose existence implies B's existence. For example, when Robinson Crusoe found the strange footprint in the sand, his knowledge of Friday's existence was indirect, since it was based on the belief that (B) some human being, not himself, must have made (A) the footprint. Since a direct proof of God's existence is, by definition, only within God's power, it is an indirect proof that Aquinas promises us. He believes that in such a proof we may infer God's existence from his function, although such a proof cannot give us a knowledge of God's divine form.

Briefly put, Aquinas's program is to show us that from the existence of certain features of the world, which he argues emanate from God, we may infer the existence of God. Now an indirect proof's power to convince us of existence can be no greater than the strength of the belief which it induces that the existence of A does imply the existence of B. Aquinas meets this criterion more than half way, by arguing that the connection between the existence of certain features of the world and God's existence is necessary, i.e. it is impossible to think of one without thinking of the other. Such a proof of God's existence will be, of course, a philosophical one, since it makes use of one of the philosopher's principal weapons of argument: You must accept my conclusion or land in a self-contradiction, a fate unbearable to any reasonable person.

Aquinas approaches the task of proving God's existence very much under the influence of the ancient Greek philosopher, Aristotle. He seems especially to have had in mind a part of Aristotle's doctrine of causes. Aristotle believed that anything could be explained by giving an account of its four different kinds of causes: its formal cause, its material cause, its efficient cause, and its final cause. His doctrine of causes may be illustrated by the following answers to the question, "What are the four causes of a bronze statue of a discus thrower?" Its formal cause, i.e. its form, is that of a man throwing a discus. Its material cause, i.e. the stuff of which it is made, is bronze. Its efficient cause, i.e. that which made it, is the sculptor. Its final cause, i.e. the end or purpose for which it was made, is more difficult to name. However, one or more of the following might be counted as the final cause or causes: the sculptor's desire to make such a statue, his desire to fill a patron's order to make such a statue, the patron's desire to display such a statue, and so on.

It is important to notice that while Aristotle seems to have conceived his doctrine of causes while thinking of artifacts, that is, man-made objects, he does not explicitly restrict its application to them. So one may come away from Aristotle with the impression that his four causal questions (What is its form? What is it made of? What made it? What is its purpose?) may be asked of anything, natural objects as well as artifacts; and this seems to be just what Aquinas did. He was particularly interested in asking of everything, "What made it?" and he seems to have accepted the dictum that for each and every thing there is an efficient cause. We are now in possession of the conceptual basis for the premise that underlies all of Aquinas's arguments to prove God's existence; and that premise is, God's existence may be inferred from certain features of the world because their existence implies God's existence as their efficient cause.

Aquinas offers five arguments to prove that God exists. Since all of the arguments are constructed in accordance with the principle of inferring God's existence from the existence of some feature of the world, the marvel is not that Aquinas was able to find five arguments, but that he stopped at five. For the number of arguments which he might have produced is limited only by the number of divinely dependent features of the world that he cared to distinguish. The examination of one of his arguments, then, should be sufficient to illustrate his method. The one I have chosen, "the second way," is the argument from "the nature of the efficient cause." The English Dominican Fathers translate Aquinas's argument from the original Latin in the following way:

The second way is from the nature of the efficient cause. In the world of sense we find there is an order of efficient causes. There is no case known (neither is it, indeed, possible) in which a thing is found to be the efficient cause of itself; for so it would be prior to itself, which is impossible. Now in efficient causes it is not possible to go on to infinity, because in all efficient causes following in order, the first is the cause of the intermediate cause, and the intermediate is the cause of the ultimate cause, whether the intermediate cause be several, or one only. Now to take away the cause is to take away the effect. Therefore, if there be no first cause among efficient causes, there will be no ultimate, nor any intermediate cause. But if in efficient causes it is possible to go on to infinity, there will be no first efficient cause, neither will there be an ultimate effect, nor any intermediate efficient causes; all of which is plainly false. Therefore it is necessary to admit a first efficient cause, to which everyone gives the name of God.[1]

To bring out the rigor of Aquinas's argument, I shall put it in a form which shows each step and its evidence. My own interpolations to provide needed premises and evidence, implied but not stated by Aquinas, are in brackets. The form in which I restate the argument may remind my readers of their geometry homework. They may recall that the proof of each proposition in geometry is headed by a construction, or geometer's picture, of what is to be proved. Can a suitable philosopher's picture be provided at the head of Aquinas's argument? Perhaps it can, if the reader will imagine the following motion picture: We see first a table top on which twenty-eight dominoes have been set on end in a column. Each domino is so close to its neighbor that if the domino at the head of the column were knocked against the one behind it, a chain reaction would be started in which the dominoes would knock each other down in series until the last one falls. A child comes to the table. With an outstretched finger he knocks the first domino into the one behind, and the whole column goes down. End of motion picture. The reader is not to identify the child with God. Rather he is to regard the whole movie as an epitome of our world in which each event has its efficient cause. And now the restatement of Aquinas's argument to prove that God exists:

[1] From the Third Article of Question II in the First Part of the *Summa Theologica*, Vol. I. Translation published and copyright by Benziger Brothers, Inc., New York, 1947.

[We are required to prove that it is necessary to admit a first efficient cause to which everyone gives the name of God.]

1. In the world of sense we find there is an order of efficient causes.

1. [Aquinas's reader is expected to consider the world in the light of Aristotle's concept of "the efficient cause," and to agree that each thing in the world must be caused by something else (e.g. as in the domino movie above).]

2. In all efficient causes following in order, the first is the cause of the intermediate cause, and the intermediate is the cause of the ultimate cause, whether the intermediate cause be several or one only.

2. [Definition, i.e. this is the way we are to talk about the order of efficient causes.]

3. If there be no first cause among efficient causes, there will be no ultimate, nor any intermediate cause.

3. To take away the cause is to take away the effect.

4. [A first efficient cause cannot be denied on the grounds that there is an infinite regress in efficient causes.]

4. If in efficient causes it is possible for there to be an infinite regress, there will be no first efficient cause, neither will there be an ultimate effect, nor any intermediate efficient cause.

5. [A first efficient cause cannot be denied on the grounds that the order of efficient causes in the world is its own cause.]

5. a. There is no case known in which a thing is found to be the efficient cause of itself.
5. b. Neither is it indeed possible. For so it would be prior to itself, which is impossible.

6. [*The only ways* of escaping accepting the existence of a first cause in the order of efficient causes are shown to be untenable by 4 and 5 above.]

6. [Aquinas's reader must satisfy himself that he can think of no alternative to explaining the existence of the order of efficient causes in the world but a first efficient cause.]

∴ It is necessary to admit a first efficient cause to which everyone gives the name of God.

The first point at which this argument is often questioned is the conclusion itself. Allowing that the argument proves the existence of a first efficient cause, does it prove the existence of God? Despite Aquinas's saying that everyone must give the first efficient cause the name of God, one may still ask, "But is this cause God? Might not the first efficient cause be something other than God, such as some fundamental characteristic of the world like the atomic structure of matter or electro-magnetism?" To these questions Aquinas would say that the first efficient cause must be God. For he does not allow that any aspect of the world can ever be the starting point of the order of efficient causes. He believes that one may always ask of any aspect of the world, "What caused it?" and finally to answer this question one must arrive at God, who by his nature transcends the world. An examination of the conclusion of this argument then brings out Aquinas's tacit assumption that only God can be the first cause in the order of efficient causes. I think that his view is fairly represented by saying that for him the statement, "God is not the first efficient cause," is as self-contradictory as saying, "Triangles do not have three angles." If we are to get anywhere at all with Aquinas's argument then we must accept his conception of God; and this now puts us in a good position to squeeze it. Does the argument prove that there must be a first efficient cause? If it fails, Aquinas is left with no chance to bring his conception of God into play.

Let us look then at the most important premises in this argument, that is the first three; and let us treat them for as long as we can as matter-of-fact statements, that is as statements which describe discoverable features of the world, notably an order of efficient causes and an efficient cause of efficient causation; and let us see if we can find these features of the world. We may begin with the claim of the first premise, which is elaborated in the second, that there is in the world of sense "an order of efficient causes." How are we to look for this order? Clearly it is not like looking for a particular thing, such as an okapi. Nor is it like looking for a particular process, such as the answer to the question of how my breakfast egg got to my plate. The order of efficient causes appears to be something more than either a thing or a process, but what more? To find it, we are reduced to asking the fundamental question, "What does the phrase 'an order of efficient causes' mean?" First of all let us ask how we use "efficient cause," or just "cause" when we mean "efficient cause." Notice that we usually talk about the cause of a particular event or the cause of a certain set of events; and we can trace out the causal history of an event or set of events. But is it true that all events or even all sets of events are causally connected in a single order of events? That all events are temporally related is a claim we need not question here. But we must not let our universal assumption of this relation confuse us. As we ordinarily talk about causes, it is not true that we expect to trace out a causal connection among all events or all sets of events. Hence Aquinas expects us to buy more than we are ready to shop for when he tries to sell us the claim that there is an order of efficient causes. "But," someone might say, "even if there is not *an* order of efficient causes, might there not be orders of efficient causes operating in parallel series, so that Aquinas's argument would still hold, because these orders of efficient causes need *an* efficient cause." Clearly such a defender of Aquinas would have to argue for a single efficient cause of the orders of efficient causes, or else his acceptance of the different orders would lead to polytheism. But even when the argument is amended in this way, have we saved it from all its difficulties? We must still ask what we are to make of the claim that there must be an efficient cause of efficient causation.

Let us look at the third premise, "If there be no first cause among efficient causes, there will be no ultimate nor any intermediate cause." Our questions must be, "Is the first cause among efficient causes something that one can look for?" and, if it is, "How does one go about looking for it?" Notice the condition which makes our talk of efficient causes intelligible. When I ask what caused something, it is a fair question only if I have left over some of the world in which the answer can be found. When I ask, "How did my breakfast egg get on my plate?" I ask only about a part of the world; and I leave over the rest of it, in which a series of agents from the cook back to the hen on her nest can be distinguished as the cause of the presence of the egg

on my plate. When I make a claim about the origin of my breakfast egg, I leave to whoever wants to disprove my claim the rest
of the world in which to search for some feature or set of features which can explain the presence of the egg on my plate
better than my claim about hens and cooks. I can afford to do
so, for I feel secure in my claim; and the price of my security is
that I must leave room for any challenge to be proved. But is the
question, "What is the first cause of efficient causes?" like "How
did my breakfast egg get on my plate?" It is not. For, if the
world is regarded either as an order of efficient causes or as a
number of such orders, what is left over in the world to be the
cause of the order or orders of efficient causes? What could I
show someone in the world to prove false the claim that there
is no efficient cause of efficient causation? By taking all efficient
causes into his claim that there is an efficient cause of efficient
causes, Aquinas has made that claim empirically meaningless.
Because they leave over a piece of the world in which their
causes may be distinguished, we can understand claims about the
efficient causes of particular events or particular series of events;
but the claim that there is an efficient cause of efficient causation
is unlike these ordinary claims. It sounds like them; but on examination it proves not to be like them. Therefore any intelligibility
which it gained by its assumed resemblance to our ordinary
talk about causes turns out to be a pseudo-intelligibility. Because
it is unintelligible, we may reject Aquinas's third premise; and by
rejecting it, we also contradict the sixth. For we have affirmed
another way of escaping the necessity of accepting a first efficient
cause, i.e. by arguing that the concept of the efficient cause of
efficient causation can be given no meaning.

But now see what has happened to Aquinas's argument. Its
appeal depended on his showing that there must be a first efficient cause, and accepting his view that this cause must be God.
The phrase, "first efficient cause," meaning the "efficient cause of
efficient causation," has, however, been shown to be empirically
meaningless; and any identification of God with these terms
makes "God" an empty word.

But at this point we may imagine someone's saying, "Too fast!

Too fast! By treating a first efficient cause as though it must be found in the world, you are trying to make Aquinas show us that God is in the world; but this is not the sort of task which it is fair to impose upon him." In reply, I can say only that I began by treating the premises of the argument as though they were matter-of-fact statements. When they are regarded as such, it is fair to see whether they are empirically meaningful; and these statements, unfortunately for Aquinas, turn out not to be so. The alternative is to treat them as matter-of-logic statements. But if we accept this alternative, the argument is hopelessly damaged. For matter-of-logic statements tell us nothing of existence. Still, it may be that Aquinas really did hope to prove God's existence by an argument consisting of matter-of-logic premises. At least, this is the conclusion one might come to by considering the question of why Aquinas thought that Aristotle's doctrine of efficient cause might have something to do with proving God's existence. For Aquinas's reliance on the doctrine apparently rests on a misunderstanding. He interprets so broadly Aristotle's claim that we may ask about the efficient cause of anything that he is prepared to seek even the efficient cause of efficient causation itself. But to understand Aristotle as claiming that everything must have an efficient cause, including efficient causation itself, is to make his doctrine prove too much. For to grant the doctrine is to grant that there must be an efficient cause of efficient causation; but to proceed in this way is to assume at the outset what the argument from efficient cause is designed to prove.

That Aquinas assumes what he wants to prove may be brought out in yet another way. While he subsumes efficient causation itself under the Aristotelian rule that everything has an efficient cause, the plausibility of his argument rests on the tacit assumption that no one will ask what caused God. If we asked, "What caused God?" we should not be talking in accordance with Aquinas's conception of God as a *first* efficient cause. Thus, for Aquinas, the doctrine of efficient cause applies to everything but God; and it is only when we agree that God is an exception to the doctrine that it appears possible to find a first efficient cause.

Perhaps knowing that Aquinas endeavors to guarantee his argument by a conceptual rule about what cannot be asked will make it easier to appreciate the defeat of his argument by a conceptual rule: that is, the rule against asking for the first efficient cause of the order of efficient causes, because of the meaninglessness of such a request.

Are these strictures on Aquinas's argument too severe? I think not, in the light of his own criticisms of another argument to prove God's existence, the ontological argument. "Ontological" is the adjective form of "ontology," which means "the knowledge, or science, of being." The ontological argument is given its name because it is a proof of God's existence drawn from the nature of God's being or essence. It is argued that God's nature is such that it necessarily implies his existence. Once someone understands this characteristic of God's nature, one can see that it is impossible to think of God without thinking of him as existing.

The version of the ontological argument which Aquinas considers is an attempt to show that the statement "God exists" is self-evident. A self-evident statement is one which someone agrees to as soon as he understands its terms. For example, the statement, "The whole is greater than any one of its parts," is agreed to as soon as one understands how the words "whole" and "part" are being used. The argument then seeks to show that the statement, "God exists," is self-evident for the following reasons:

1. ". . . it is possible to think that something exists whose non-existence cannot be thought.

2. "Clearly, such a being is greater than the being whose non-existence can be thought.

3. "Consequently, if God Himself could be thought not to be, then something greater than God could be thought.

4. "The above statement, however, is contrary to the definition of the name God.

"Hence, the proposition that God exists is self-evident." [2]

[2] From *On the Truth of the Catholic Faith, Book One: God,* by St. Thomas Aquinas, translated by Anton Pegis, pp. 79-80. Copyright 1955 by Doubleday and Company, Inc., reprinted by permission.

A look at this argument shows that if the statement, "God exists," is self-evident, then the words "God" and "exists" must be defined in such a way that one cannot think the statement, "God does not exist," just as one cannot think, "The whole is less than any one of its parts." The third and fourth premises imply the required definition of "God" as "that which *cannot* be thought not to be." Consequently, if one accepts this definition of "God," one must say, "God exists." But this is the very point at which Aquinas attacks this kind of argument. If its success turns on our accepting a certain definition of "God," then the argument can be made to fail simply by our refusing to accept the definition. There is nothing which compels us to accept this particular definition of "God." There are many ways of conceiving of God. So all this argument does is show us one way of thinking of God. But as Aquinas points out, defining a word is not the same operation as showing that the thing which the word names does exist. To drive Aquinas's point home: I can tell you that "unicorn" means "a horselike creature with a single, long, pointed horn in the middle of its forehead," but my definition of "unicorn" is not to be confused with the claim that unicorns exist. My being able to define the word does not rule out the possibility of your asking, "Are there unicorns?" and waiting to be shown.

Now what can be said of Aquinas's own argument to prove God's existence, in the light of his criticism of the ontological argument? Just as the ontological argument turns on a particular conception of God, so Aquinas's argument turns on a particular conception of the world, i.e. as an order of efficient causes in need of a first efficient cause. If the ontological argument fails to prove God's existence conclusively because it depends on the acceptance of a particular conception, so Aquinas's argument to prove God's existence fails because it relies on our conceiving of the world as in need of a first efficient cause. What is more, our rejection of this conception of the world is not arbitrary, or simply a matter of taste, for we have shown it to be meaningless.

I have limited myself to an examination of only one of Aquinas's five arguments to prove God's existence. But my claim is that when the other four are subjected to a similar examination, they will be seen to depend on conceiving the world in a certain way; and they fail to prove God's existence when one refuses to think of the world as the arguments dictate. Whether the particular conceptions of the world which the other four arguments require are meaningless, as the conception required by the second argument is, is a question which I must leave to the reader's own examination.

## DOES EVIL PROVE GOD'S NON-EXISTENCE?

The argument that the existence of evil in the world proves that God does not exist in heaven or anywhere else is a curious mirror image of Aquinas's style of argument. Aquinas argued that the existence of certain features of the world entitle us to infer that God exists. In the argument from evil it is argued that existence of a certain feature of the world entitles us to infer that God does not exist. The argument rests on two assumptions. The first is that God must be both benevolent and omnipotent. The second is that the presence of evil in the world would be contrary to the governance of the world by a benevolent and omnipotent God. When the contention that there is evil in the world is added to these assumptions, God's existence is thought to be disproved.

The Baron d'Holbach states the argument from evil in the following way:

It is more than two thousand years, since, according to Lactantius, the sage Epicurus observed: "either God would remove evil out of this world, and cannot; or he can, and will not; or he has not the power nor will; or, lastly, he has both the power and will. If he has the will, and not the power, this shows weakness, which is contrary to the nature of God. If he has the power, and not the will, it is malignity; and this is no less contrary to his nature. If he is neither able nor willing, he is both impotent and malignant, and consequently cannot be God. If he be both willing and able (which alone is consonant to the nature of God) whence comes evil, or why does he not prevent it?" Reflecting minds have been waiting a reasonable solution of these difficulties, for more than two thousand years; and our divines tell us, that they will be removed only in a future life. . . .[3]

[3] From *Common Sense* by Paul Thyry, Baron d'Holbach, 4th edition, 1856.

The alternatives open to someone who wants to offer a reasonable reply to the argument from evil are these: He can attack the conception of God on which the argument rests; or he can try to reduce the importance to be found in the presence of evil in the world. The first alternative is not a real one for a Christian, because no Christian wants to deny that God is both benevolent and omnipotent; and it is to be supposed that all serious theists, troubled by the argument from evil, would join Christians in their stand, rather than say that God is either malevolent or impotent or both. If any reply is to be made to the argument, then, it must be made on the lines of the second alternative.

Is there evil in the world? And if there is, does it count against God's benevolence and omnipotence? In the first place, it must be admitted quite frankly that "evil" is a slippery term. Things can be evil; but evil itself is not a thing. Calling something evil then depends on the way you look at it. On first consideration one might think that one could answer the question, "What is evil?" by saying something like "Pain, pestilence, and poverty." But paradoxically pain and pestilence keep physicians in business; so they find some good in what the rest of mankind finds a burden. As for poverty, while the have-nots may count it an evil, any haves whose prosperity depends on it may think differently. The relativity of judgments about what is evil, then, may be used to provide opponents of the argument from evil with ways of diminishing its force.

Three replies to the argument based on reducing the importance of evil appear to be possible:

(1) When someone says that evil counts against God's benevolence and omnipotence, we may ask, "How do you know that there is evil in the world?" Remember that your measure of evil is human and not divine. If you could only see the world as God does, you would know that what you count as evil is only part of the divine harmony of the whole world. It is true that your mosquito bite may itch, and that from time to time a mosquito may succumb to your swats. But what are a few of your mosquito bites or a few squashed mosquitoes to God, when he can contemplate the harmony of a whole which includes mosqui-

toes biting people and people swatting mosquitoes? On this view, then, the force of the argument from evil can be dissipated by replying that evil is not really evil when one takes a divinely synoptic view of the world.

(2) When someone claims that evil counts against God's omnipotence and benevolence, it may be replied that evil is really a good, through serving a necessary function in the world. If there were no evil, we should not know how to identify the good, or feel any desire to seek it, because the good is only good by contrast with evil. If there were no opposite to good, we should never have any occasion to call anything good. If we never experienced any evil, we should never feel pushed to acquire the good. Thus it is really a piece of benevolence on God's part that there is evil in the world.

(3) The third effort to diminish the importance of evil in the world is to claim that evil is beneath man's notice. We have here the Christian doctrine that the evil which we suffer in this life is of no consequence when we consider the heavenly bliss that may be ours in the next life. It is not to be supposed that suffering alone is a passport to a heavenly future. It must be combined with Christian faith. But for this reply to the argument from evil to be taken seriously, the attribution of benevolence to God is necessarily qualified. It must be admitted that God's benevolence does not extend to the world in a uniform fashion. It is known at its best only in heaven. On this view, then, the evil in this world is admitted, but it is not allowed to count against God's benevolence.

Having looked at both the argument from evil and possible replies, can we say either that the argument disproves God's existence or that the replies destroy the argument's effectiveness? The alternative we choose appears to depend on our point of view. Measles disprove God's existence for you if you say they do. Measles do not disprove his existence if you say that they do not. Clearly, then, the argument from evil, and the replies which may be made to it, settle nothing. One takes one's pick as one wishes pre-existing notions to be shored up. But such a state of affairs only shows that the conclusion of the argument, and all counter claims, are matter-of-logic statements. We are so far from questions of existence here that we can have no hope of learning anything about God, although we can learn a great deal about the minds of people who believe or disbelieve in him.

While matter-of-logic arguments must of necessity fail to answer the question of God's existence one way or the other, we may nonetheless hope that some empirical considerations might be advanced to show whether or not God exists. Miracles have long formed the basis for such considerations; and it is to this topic that I now wish to turn.

## Do Miracles Prove God's Existence?

Our first question must be, "What is a miracle?" A religious person would tell us that it is an event whose occurrence could not be explained if God were not its cause. Here then is a rule for distinguishing miracles from all other events and we must see whether it can be applied. It is important to notice that if someone says that every event is a miracle, he removes any distinctive meaning from the word "miracle." It means simply "event."

Our second question is, "What characteristics must an event have in order for us to agree that God caused it?" We must be certain that no other causal agency can explain the event. It appears, then, that a miracle must be an event which happens in the absence of a natural cause, for only then could we be certain that no causal agency but God could explain its occurrence. Notice that a miracle must not be merely wonderful. That is, we must not count as a miracle an event that is highly improbable but nonetheless possible, as, for example, a remarkable medical cure which the physician thought there was little chance of effecting, but in whose accomplishment he nonetheless employed all his knowledge and energy. Nor must we count as a miracle an event whose cause we do not know, simply because we are ignorant of the cause. Our own ignorance must not be taken as a sign that no cause can be found. In short, neither our wonder at the occurrence of an event nor our ignorance of its cause must be mistaken for proof that a miracle has happened.

Our third question must be, "Could we ever tell that an event has occurred in the absence of a natural cause?" If we can tell, then we can say that God has caused a miracle. But how can we tell that an event has happened in the absence of a natural cause? Our knowledge of nature is a knowledge of the usual causes of events. Without such knowledge, we should have no reason to suspect that an event had occurred in the absence of its natural cause. But notice the fatal effect of such knowledge. Once we have a set of firm expectations about a given causal connection, it is reasonable to suppose that when a given event occurs it happens as the result of its usual cause. This is not to say that we cannot conceive of an event's happening as the result of a different cause; but if a certain kind of event did happen as the result of more than one kind of cause, we should simply enlarge our list of the possible usual causes of such an event. What we cannot conceive is an event's happening in the absence of any natural cause. Now the proponent of miracles will rightly say that he does not expect us to conceive of events happening without any cause at all. He expects us to admit no more than the possibility of events which we must attribute to a supernatural cause. But we can only make room for supernatural causes if we are in a position to rule out all natural causes of some event. For the proponent of miracles to make his case, he must persuade us that an event has happened first in the absence of its usual cause and second in the absence of any other natural cause. But who is to say when the search for a natural cause should stop? In effect, we are saying that "cause" means "natural cause," and we could never have a use for the phrase "supernatural cause." It is no wonder then that even when we have not seen a cause operate, we find it more reasonable to suppose that an event is the result of its usual cause rather than that it happened in the absence of any cause at all.

An example will enforce the point. At the marriage feast in Cana (John 2:1-11), Jesus is said to have turned water into wine. Now if this story were true, it would mean that wine had been produced in the absence of its usual cause, that is, grape juice given time to ferment. But I ask the reader which is more likely:

that Jesus did turn water into wine, or that something like the following chain of events happened. On being invited to the feast, Jesus orders his disciples to buy a few jars of wine to take along, because he knows how an extra jar of wine always comes in handy at parties. When Jesus and his disciples arrive at the party, their host is so occupied in greeting the foremost members of the group that he does not see that some of the men at the back put down some jars in the dark corner just inside the door. When the wine supply runs out and Jesus calls for the waterpots to be filled with water, it is one of Jesus's disciples who recognizes a signal and passes the servants the jars of wine waiting in the dark corner. From these jars the servants fill the waterpots. To the company's amazement, it is wine that the servants then pour from the waterpots, and superior wine at that. (It is often the case that someone who buys a little wine for a present spends more than someone who is buying a lot of wine for a big party.) Notice that it takes many more words to describe what might have happened than it does to say that Jesus turned water into wine. Of any account of an event which is supposed to have happened in the absence of its usual cause, we may always ask, "What has been left out of the story?"

In the light of the above considerations, it may be asked why miracles come to be reported. One answer often given is that mankind takes great delight in being mystified and that the re-tailers of miracles are catering to this desire. A harsher answer which is sometimes given is that stories of miracles are deliberate frauds designed to enthrall the ignorant for the profit of the story-telling rascals. But whether entertainment or fraud be their purpose, the antidote to miracle stories is considering a given story against that piece of causal knowledge which would have to be ignored in order for the story to be true, and deciding whether its absence is more probable than its presence.

I cannot leave this subject without remarking that the famous Christian apologist, Professor C. S. Lewis, thinks that a Christian can admit the occurrence of such a miracle as the resurrection of Jesus, because it is fitting to the nature of God that he perform this miracle. But this is to remove the question of miracles from the area of empirical considerations and to base their likelihood on one's conception of God. As we have already seen in this chapter, any conclusion can be shown to follow from the proper set of conceptions, but the empirical truth of the conclusion must be shown by experience. Interestingly enough, Professor Lewis's position is exactly countered by Spinoza. He thought that it was eminently *unfitting* to attribute miracles to God, because he conceived of God as being supremely rational. Any disturbance in the order of nature would show that God had changed his mind about his plans for nature. But to suppose that such a change of mind could occur in God would be to contradict the idea of his supreme rationality. Hence, neither can God be thought of as an author of miracles, nor ought the truly religious to expect him to be.

This examination of the topic of miracles, then, makes it doubtful that they can be cited to prove God's existence. Empirically we have no way of identifying events that have happened in the absence of a natural cause. So far as conceptions of the divine go, miracles can be either allowed or not allowed to occur. Thus our thoughts can do nothing to remove the doubts raised by empirical considerations.

## RELIGION, EXPERIENCE, AND FAITH

At this point we should do well to remember that there are a good many people in the world who believe that there is a god, and who regard themselves as having very good reasons for doing so. Their reasons are not at all the careful kind of philosopher's argument which Aquinas offers. In some vague sense their reasons are thought to be empirical; but they are not so in a sufficiently clear-cut way to enable us to meet them head on with the objections which can be made against appeals to miracles. So more work is needed to elucidate the popular claim that God can be experienced. This claim can be dealt with only by considering each case as it is met. All that I can do here is consider several cases which I take to be illustrative of their kind, and show what a philosopher can say about them. By this means I hope to sketch at least the outlines of what it is for someone to have religious faith, and the effect of faith on the interpretation of experience.

But lest I be thought to be legislating a meaning for the word "faith," let me say that I am considering only one of its meanings, and let me distinguish that meaning from those with which it might be confused. We sometimes say of someone, "I have faith in him," meaning that we trust him, and that we shall do so despite evidence that makes him appear to be untrustworthy. There is a closely related use of "faith" in religious talk, wherein a person says that he believes some statement without evidence; and he is prepared to believe without evidence, because he does not see how he is to obtain it. Many people, and I suspect particularly the irreligious, believe that this last use of "faith" is the only one appropriate to a religious context; and consequently the religious are ridiculed for believing that which they know not why they believe. Whereupon the religious turn the other cheek and glory in their believing without the justification that ordinary mortals cry after.

There is, however, another use of "faith" which I believe is more important to religion; and to miss it is to miss most of what religion is. This use may be seen in such phrases as "the Christian faith" or "the Jewish faith" or the comparable phrase, "my faith." "Faith" here means a set of doctrines or beliefs; and the person who holds them need not necessarily subscribe to them without being prepared to support them by appeals to evidence or good reasons. It is this last sense of "faith" which I wish to discuss; and I want to show that it amounts to holding an interpretive point of view by means of which otherwise natural events may be made to have religious significance.

One of the most famous experiments to prove the existence of God must be the contest between Elijah and the prophets of Baal. The story may be found in the Bible in I Kings (18:20-40). Elijah deliberately sets out to prove that "the Lord" exists and that Baal does not. He puts the issue squarely to the Israelites, when he says, "How long halt ye between two opinions, if the LORD *be* God, follow him: but if Baal, then follow him." He proposes the fol-

lowing test to settle the issue: "Let them therefore give us two
bullocks; and let them choose one bullock for themselves, and
cut it in pieces, and lay it on wood, and put no fire under: and
I will dress the other bullock, and lay it on wood, and put no fire
under: and call ye on the name of your gods, and I will call on
the name of the Lord: and the god that answereth by fire, let
him be God." The prophets of Baal take their turn at calling;
but no fire lights their altar. Elijah adds to their discomfiture by
ridiculing their god: "Cry aloud for he *is* a god; either he is talking, or he is pursuing, or he is on a journey, or peradventure he
sleepeth, and must be awakened." Finally it is Elijah's turn to
try; and he heightens interest in the contest by soaking with
water the offering, the wood, the altar, and the surrounding
ground, until water even stands in a trench that has been dug
around the Lord's altar. I think we may take it that Elijah has
concealed no fire-originating material on or about the altar that
is either immediately operable by itself or remotely operable by
him. When all is ready, Elijah calls on the Lord to "let it be
known that thou art God in Israel, and that I am thy servant,
and that I have done all these things at thy word. . . . Then
the fire of the LORD fell, and consumed the burnt sacrifice, and
the wood, and the stones, and the dust, and licked up the water
that was in the trench. And when all the people saw it, they fell
on their faces: and they said, the LORD, he *is* the God; the
LORD, he *is* the God." [4]

Now what are we to make of this story? A good question to

---

[4] The proposal for a modern parallel to Elijah's contest is reported in *The
New York Times,* March 5, 1960, page 4. Reprinted by permission.

MOSLEM DARES GRAHAM TO COMPETE IN HEALING

NAIROBI, Kenya, March 4 (AP)—The Rev. Dr. Billy Graham was challenged
today to a healing contest to see whether Christianity is more powerful than
Islam.

On his return to Nairobi from Ruanda-Urundi on his African trip, the evan-
gelist was handed a letter from the chief of the Ahmadiyya Moslem mission in
East Africa, Maulana Sheikh Mubarak Ahmad.

Contending that Islam alone is the living religion on earth through which man
can attain salvation and that Christianity is utterly devoid of any heavenly bless-
ing or true guidance for man, the letter suggested that "thirty incurables" be
certified by the director of medical services of Kenya and "be equally divided
between you and me by lots."

"We may then be joined by six persons of our respective faiths in prayer to start with is, how are we to understand the phrase, "the fire of the LORD fell"? From its effect, there can be no doubt about the existence of the fire; and from its being said to fall, I should judge that "the fire of the LORD" was a bolt of lightning. If someone wants to argue that it was not a bolt of lightning or some other natural kind of fire but a fire that was in some sense supernatural, we should have to ask how one tells the difference between these two kinds of fire. If the difference is an inherent one, I must leave it to the proponent of supernatural fire to explain how one can distinguish between the two kinds. If, as I suspect, the difference is only an occasional one, then the question of how one identifies an instance of supernatural fire is open to the same kind of answer as the question of how one determines that a particular bolt of lightning had a divine origin. How could we tell that Elijah's particular bolt of lightning came from the Lord? What distinguishes this bolt of lightning from all other bolts? Judging by the story, the answer is that it struck in a particular place at a particular time. But is this criterion sufficient to satisfy us that Elijah's particular bolt of lightning came from God? There are some supplementary questions which intrude at this point.

(1) What would Elijah have said if a bolt of lightning had struck Baal's altar? From the terms of the contest, it appears that he would have had to admit that Baal exists.

(2) What would Elijah have said if bolts of lightning had struck both altars, first Baal's and later the Lord's? From the terms of the contest, it appears that the existence of both gods would have been proved.

(3) What would Elijah have said if lightning had struck neither altar? From the terms of the contest, it appears that he would have had to admit that neither god existed.

Now what light do these remarks throw on the question of whether right time and place are sufficient criteria to enable us to tell that Elijah's bolt of lightning is of divine origin? Notice that

God for the recovery of our respective patients to determine as to who is blessed with the Lord's grace and mercy and upon whom His door remains closed," the letter added.

Dr. Graham declined comment and one of his associates said it was doubtful he would make any reply.

the answer to each of the earlier questions contains the phrase
"from the terms of the contest." The terms define the right time
and place; and the lightning bolt may be said to be from the
Lord because it fits the terms. There is nothing inherent in the
lightning bolt which enables us to discern its divine quality.
Rather it is its previously defined occasion which is the clue. But
what then can we say about Elijah's proof of the Lord's existence? It is a proof only for those who look at it as Elijah instructs.
There is nothing inherent in the reported events that proves
God's existence. They prove it when we read them aright. To
the uninstructed, the all-important flash of divine fire is just another bolt of lightning; and Elijah was lucky to have it strike his
pile of rocks.

To illustrate to the full the character of Elijah's proof, let me
show how his own method may be used to disprove the existence
of God. I am told that the great American atheist Robert G.
Ingersoll used sometimes to finish his orations against religion
by pulling out his watch and saying that if there is a god, he dared
that god to strike him dead within the next three minutes. Ingersoll would then hold his watch in his hand and impassively count
off the minutes. At the end of the appointed time he would snap
his watch shut, and sit down wearing a triumphant smile.

It is important to see that during his act, Ingersoll was only a
kind of negative Elijah. His act proved that God does not exist,
because that is the way he looked at it, just as Elijah's contest
proved that the Lord exists, because that is the way he looked at
it. But the philosopher must ask, "What would Ingersoll's followers have said if he had dropped dead one night? What would
Elijah have said if the lightning had not fallen?"

In this discussion of Elijah and his reverse image, Ingersoll, I
have been endeavoring to show that it is only by taking a con-
sciously interpretive view of natural events that they may be
made to serve as evidence of the divine. Someone's religious faith
is his having such an interpretive view, and his applying it in
the interpretation of natural events. It follows from such an account of faith that, while statements made on faith have the look
of matter-of-fact statements, they are really matter-of-logic in char-

acter. Elijah can say, "The lightning's striking my altar proves the Lord's existence," and the arrival of the lightning bolt looks like empirical confirmation of his statement. Looks so, until we remember that we see the lightning bolt as a divine sign because we have learned our lesson. We have no way of seeing it as such without the lesson; and having to learn this kind of lesson makes the statement matter-of-logic. This matter-of-logic character of statements made on faith would be confirmed if those people who regarded them as true would count their contradictories as uninteresting, or irrelevant, or even meaningless. We do not know what Elijah would have said if the lightning bolt had not struck his altar; so my example can provide no material for our consideration, and I must ask the reader to test my claim against any examples of faith that he might meet. But I am inclined to think that if the lightning had not struck his altar, Elijah would never have said, "Since the lightning did not strike my altar, the Lord does not exist," even though the terms of the contest suggest that he should say this. Rather, he would say that the failure, interpreted in accordance with other aspects of his faith, proves either that he was unfit to be the Lord's prophet or, perhaps more characteristically, that the Lord had rejected the Israelites because of their unworthiness. Similarly with regard to what might be called Ingersoll's irreligious faith, if he had dropped dead during one of his divine challenges, his adherents would have said not that it proved that a god exists, but rather that Ingersoll had a bad heart, counting it as a "perfectly natural" cause of death. Given the matter-of-logic character of faith, then, Elijah's contest to prove the Lord's existence is closer to Aquinas's reasonable arguments than a plain believer might at first suppose. But while plain believers have a very good reason for claiming that what they say about God on the basis of faith is true, the reason is not empirical evidence, as they might suppose, but rather the matter-of-logic character of their statements.

I want to round out this account of faith by examining a little more closely the way in which the holding of an interpretive point of view can turn an experience into a religious experience. For our purposes it would be best to discuss the plainest sort of

experience that can still be called a religious experience, for only
then can we get at the workings of religious faith as it appears
in the lives of millions of people. Too often a discussion of religious experience starts at the level of visions or remarkable feelings, occurrences far away from the lives of most people; and
then the debunkers are let in to have their day. St. Paul is written off as an epileptic. St. Bernadette only suffered a hallucina-
tion which accompanied an attack of vertigo brought on by
stooping to gather firewood under a hot sun. And so this sort
of comment goes on, until we have William James saying, "In
point of fact, the religious are often neurotic." [5] Or worse yet,
if the religious people of the world are not counted as mad, they
are dismissed as crooks, and sometimes as both. Thus, religious
experience is too easily explained away without even touching
its character in the lives of those to whom nothing is more important than their religion.

As an example of the plain sort of religious experience which
we ought to consider, I offer the following extracts from a Grand
Vicar's notes on his conversations with a seventeenth-century
friar, Brother Lawrence:

> . . . He told me that God had done him a singular favor, in his
> conversion at the age of eighteen.
> That in the winter, seeing a tree stripped of its leaves, and consider-
> ing that within a little time the leaves would be renewed, and after
> that the flowers and fruit appear, he received a high view of the provi-
> dence and power of God, which has never since been effaced from his
> soul. That this view had perfectly set him loose from the world, and
> kindled in him such a love of God, he could not tell whether it had
> increased during the more than forty years he had lived since.[6]

Brother Lawrence's religious experience here described is of a
fundamental sort, that of adopting the interpretive point of view
from which he will regard the rest of his experience; and this
fundamental sort of religious experience is properly called "a

---

[5] *Varieties of Religious Experience*. This sentence occurs in the Table of Con-
tents, under Lecture I, as one of the summary headings. The point is treated at
length in the lecture.

[6] *Brother Lawrence, His Conversations and Letters on the Practice of the Presence of God* (The Forward Movement, Cincinnati, Ohio), 1941, p. 5.

conversion." Lawrence comes to regard everything that is or will be as stemming from the providence and power of God. We may ask why he came to adopt this point of view; and we have his answer, that he looked at a barren tree and thought of how it would again be in leaf, and this thought led him to his "high view" of the providence and power of God. Notice how that barren tree gives the appearance of an empirical confirmation of God's providence. But do not miss the circularity of Lawrence's reasoning. He casts about him with God's providence in mind, and the barren tree confirms it.

By his conversion, Lawrence's whole way of life was transformed, so that every experience became a religious experience. He carried on his job as a cook, practicing the presence of God, turning "the cake that is frying on the pan for love of Him." [7] Or again, "It is enough for me to pick up but a straw from the ground for the love of God." [8]

Particularly illustrative of Lawrence's faith is his calling on God and receiving divine assistance. "That when an occasion of practising some virtue offered, he addressed himself to God, saying, *Lord I cannot do this unless Thou enablest me;* and that then he received strength more than sufficient." [9]

Now we may ask ourselves, would Lawrence's failing to be virtuous prove that divine providence is not responsible for everything? The answer comes, "That when he had failed in his duty, he simply confessed his fault, saying to God, *I shall never do otherwise if Thou leavest me to myself; it is Thou who must hinder my falling, and mend what is amiss.* That after this he gave himself no further uneasiness about it." [10] Lawrence's faith is sophisticated enough to make God responsible for his faults as well as his virtues. Hence, the scope of divine providence is maintained on all sides. I think Lawrence's way of life is a fair instance of the place of a religious, interpretive point of view in the life of an ordinarily religious person. It may be objected that Brother Lawrence is an extreme case, because he endeavored

---

[7] Ibid. p. 19.
[8] Ibid. p. 19.
[9] Ibid. p. 8.
[10] Ibid. pp. 8-9.

to practice the presence of God at all times. This is not, however, an uncommon ideal among religious persons, and the thoroughness with which Lawrence managed to carry it out must not be allowed to count against his typicalness.

The lesson that religious faith is but seeing events from an interpretive point of view may be confirmed by considering the word of a once faithful person who is able to stand back and take a critical look at his faith. As my last example, then, I offer an extract from the autobiography of Charles Darwin. In an arrangement unusual for English schoolboys, Darwin was sent to a public school in the same town in which his family lived, so that in his free periods during the day he was able to run home for short visits. But he was, of course, obliged to be back at school at the proper times; and he writes, "I remember in the early part of my school life that I often had to run very quickly to be in time, and from being a fleet runner was generally successful; but when in doubt I prayed earnestly to God to help me and I well remember that I attributed my success to the prayers and not to my quick running, and marvelled how generally I was aided." [11] The illustrative force of this extract will be considerably reinforced when one compares it with Brother Lawrence's account of how he is able to be virtuous by divine assistance.

By examining the foregoing illustrations from the lives of Brother Lawrence and Darwin, I have endeavored to analyze the place of faith in the lives of ordinary people, not given to the visions and transports usually associated with religious experience. The little more which I want to say is that it does not seem to me to be the job of a philosopher to recommend a particular religious faith, or to advise people in a general way about the wisdom of adopting a religious point of view. The philosopher's job is to show what religious faith is. That it is the adoption of an interpretive point of view must make no difference that would not be equally fatal to the validity of metaphysics, the natural sciences, morality, politics, and aesthetics. But whether there is

[11] *The Autobiography of Charles Darwin*, ed. by Nora Barlow (New York, Harcourt, Brace), 1959, p. 25.

any value in the adoption of a religious point of view and what sort of value it is are personal questions which each of us must decide for himself.

## SUGGESTIONS FOR FURTHER READING

In the *Summa Contra Gentiles* (published as *On the Truth of the Catholic Faith* by Image Books), Book One, Chapters 1 through 13, St. Thomas Aquinas covers in an expository way the same topics that he covers in an argumentative way in the *Summa Theologica,* First Part, Questions 1 and 2.

In *Miracles: A Preliminary Study* by C. S. Lewis (Association Press, Reflection Books), Professor Lewis both attacks Hume's argument against miracles and offers his own defense of their possibility. Spinoza's argument against miracles is to be found in the "Tractatus Theologico-Politicus," Chapter VI "Of Miracles," in *Chief Works,* Vol. I (Dover).

For an understanding of religious experience, one must be ready to collect relevant biographical material as it comes to hand. The following autobiographies are especially recommended: *Father and Son, A Study of Two Temperaments,* by Edmund Gosse (Scribner, New York, 1907); and *Memories of a Catholic Girlhood* by Mary McCarthy (Harcourt, Brace, New York, 1957). In Miss McCarthy's book, see particularly the section "C'est le Premier Pas qui Coute." Two recent examinations of religious experience especially worthy of consideration are *Religious Belief* by C. B. Martin (Cornell, Ithaca, 1959) and *Our Experience of God* by H. D. Lewis (Macmillan, New York, 1959).

Three short, modern treatments of the themes discussed in this chapter, which are much admired by each author's followers, are *Religion in the Making* by Alfred North Whitehead (Meridian), *A Common Faith* by John Dewey (Yale), and *Dynamics of Faith* by Paul Tillich (Harper Torchbooks).

## FIVE

The following items are suggested for joint reading with this chapter: *Nicomachean Ethics* by Aristotle, Bk. III, Ch. 1-5, a discussion of free actions, deliberation, and choice; *A Treatise of Human Nature* by David Hume, Bk. II, Part III, Sections I-II "Of Liberty and Necessity" in *Hume's Moral and Political Philosophy*, edited by H. D. Aiken (Hafner); *Ethics* by G. E. Moore, Ch. VI "Free Will" (Oxford University Press, New York, 1947); *The Concept of Mind* by Gilbert Ryle, Ch. III "The Will" (Barnes and Noble); and *Ethics* by Patrick Nowell-Smith, Ch. 19-20 "Freedom and Responsibility" (Penguin).

# Philosophy and Man: Human Freedom

## THE MEANING OF "FREE"

In order to be able to discuss morals and politics one must be able to suppose that it makes sense to say that people are free to act. For if there is no sense in which someone can act freely, if we must always say that whatever people do, they had to do it; that is, they could not have done otherwise, then how can we hold people responsible for what they do? How can we praise and blame? How can we reward and punish? Without supposing that people are free, we can do none of these things. My claim is that it does make sense to talk of human freedom, that is, that instances of human freedom are certainly describable. I shall try to establish this claim by answering the philosophical question, "What does it mean to say that someone is free?" and not the empirical question, "Are there any people who are free?" But the importance of the philosophical question may be gauged by the fact that until it is answered, we cannot proceed to answer the empirical question.

When can we say that someone acts freely and when can we say that he does not? What is the difference between acting freely and not acting freely? The difference is brought out by considering when we can say of someone's actions, "He could have acted otherwise." When someone has acted freely he could have done otherwise. If he could not have done otherwise, then his action was not free. To understand what it is to act freely, then, we need to make a list of the kinds of excuses which someone might offer to explain why he did not act otherwise. Typical excuses may be collected under the following heads: Lack of Knowledge (I couldn't throw the switch that turns off the motor, because I don't know anything about machinery); Lack of Ability (I couldn't save the drowning man, because I can't swim); Lack of Means (I can't buy you a ride on the carousel, because I don't have the money); Physical Fault (I couldn't reach the top shelf, because I'm not tall enough. Or, somewhat differently, I couldn't think straight, because I was ill); Psychological Fault (I can't sleep in a feather bed, because I am terrified of feathers); Threats (I had to sign the check. He was holding a pistol to my head); Force (I had to leave the night club. The bouncer was giving me the bum's rush). My claim is that whenever an instance, or some combination of instances, of these factors, or others like them, is operative, we may agree that the person so hindered could not have done otherwise. We may assess someone's freedom, then, relative to these factors; and we may say that his freedom increases in proportion to the extent of his knowledge, abilities and means, the excellence of his health and mental balance, and his fearlessness in the face of threats and force.

At this point someone might say, "It's all very well to talk of the absence of impeding factors as the clue to freedom of action. But you have not touched the internal question. For I want to ask, 'Even when there are no impediments, are people really free to act?' I won't be satisfied until you can show me that people are free *to choose* the way in which they act." How can it be shown that people are free to choose?

The question, "Are people free to choose?" may be dealt with in a way similar to that in which we dealt with "Are people free to act?" When someone is said to have made a choice, we ask, "Could he have chosen otherwise?" If the answer is "No," then, of course, he had no choice, for the essence of choosing is being able to decide otherwise; and if there is no choice, then there is no freedom. On the other hand, if the answer to "Could he have chosen otherwise?" is "Yes," then his choice was free. How then can we show that someone could have chosen otherwise? We show freedom of choice at the same time that we show freedom of action. For we show freedom of action at a given time by showing that other lines of action are open. The person did not have to act as he did. He could have done otherwise. But showing that other lines of action are open is showing that other choices might have been made; and this is what we mean by saying that a person is free to choose.

It may be objected that this account of freedom to choose is unsatisfactory because it is only an external account of the matter. Nothing has been said about what goes on inside the person making the choice. But is there an *act* of choosing that someone performs inside himself before he performs overtly those acts which he had chosen to do? Notice that if there were such an internal act of choosing, then choosing itself would be an act that one must choose to do; so before someone could choose to act, he would have to choose to choose to act. But before he could make that choice, he would have to choose to choose to choose to act. It can be seen that such a doctrine of choice would require an infinite regress of choices; and it would then be impossible for a person ever to get around to performing some action besides choosing. Of necessity, choosing to choose is a task that he could never complete. Such considerations must persuade us to forswear any search for an internal act of choosing which must privately precede any of a person's public acts.

But each of us does say, "I choose . . ." from time to time; so we must ask what we might mean when we do so. However it is used, "I choose . . ." is not used to describe an action in the way in which I may describe myself firing a gun by saying as I fire the gun, "I fire the gun." First, notice that saying, "I choose . . ." may itself be the making of a choice, as when someone says, and says truly, at the beginning of a game, "I choose Johnny to be on my side." But this use of "I choose . . ." in choosing sides or in choosing items from a list is not quite like the use of "I choose . . ." in talking about choosing a line of action. For when someone says, and says truly, "I choose to study tonight rather than go to the movies," his saying this is his starting to act in a way that will culminate in his spending the evening in study. This last use of "I choose . . ." is closely related to saying, "I choose . . ." as an announcement of what someone is going to do at a later time, as when someone says to his lawyer, "I choose to leave my money to found a cat and dog hospital." It is this use of "I choose . . ." where a considerable lapse of time between the announcement and its fulfillment is possible that may especially give rise to the belief that there must be a private act of choice which precedes our public acts. But the proper interpretation of this use of "I choose . . ." is to regard the making of the announcement as the beginning of the announced act. Thus, when someone says to his lawyer, "I choose to leave my money to found a cat and dog hospital," he has begun the act of delivering his money to a foundation. In this example, of course, his executors must complete the action for him.

To conclude this discussion of the meaning of "free," I wish to notice first a paradox of human freedom and then two notions that often becloud our thoughts about human freedom. The paradox is that the exercise of one's freedom to act limits one's freedom of action. Acting in one way at a given time precludes acting in some other way at the same time. When someone addresses himself to the study of medicine, for example, his energies are not free to be employed in any other activity of comparable magnitude. In return for the present limitation on his freedom to act, however, he gains an increment of freedom to act in the future. For when he has successfully completed his medical studies, he will be free to act as a physician. Notice, of course, that someone who has qualified himself to be a physician is unqualified, through lack of knowledge and training, to undertake many other occupations. While he is free to be a physician, in virtue of that freedom, he is not free to be a lot of other things. This example brings us to the first of the notions that may becloud our thoughts about human freedom that I wish to consider: the notion that the person who never chooses to act is freer than someone who is following out a chosen line of action.

It might be thought that the greatest freedom one can have is freedom of choice. For what greater freedom can one have than to have a wide range of choices and the freedom to choose any one of them; and the way to continue enjoying this great freedom would be never to choose at all. For as soon as one chooses, one is limited to the chosen line of action; and to limit oneself is to lessen one's freedom. But to take such a position is to forget that a person who makes no choices ceases to be a person. Living is choosing, and the advantage in finally choosing to act is that one may carry oneself to a new horizon of choices. It is true that when one chooses one occupation over all others, one restricts one's field of choice. But that occupation may contain within itself a range of choices unavailable to those who do not choose it; and, what is more, it may offer a new range of choices at each stage of one's progress in it. This is not to deny that some choices may lead to dead ends, for the price of freedom is that one must run the risk of losing it. But a freedom of choice which is un-exercised is itself a restriction of freedom, for to fail to choose is to cut oneself off from lines of action which lead to other op-portunities to choose. Indeed, to refrain steadfastly from choosing is finally to choose to be nothing.

The second notion which may becloud our thoughts of human freedom that I wish to notice is the claim that no human being can be said to be free, because no one is free not to be a human being. But it is part of being human that one is free only to be a human being. Indeed, talk of a human being's freedom to be or not to be human is nonsense, because for him to be otherwise than human would be for him to cease to be a human being. Where something cannot be otherwise than what it is and still be, there can be no question of its freedom to be otherwise than what it is. We must count being human, then, as defining the conditions for human freedom; but it would be paradoxical to count these conditions as destroying human freedom.

It may be seen that questions about whether a given person is free must always be asked with respect to a given occasion or set of occasions in his life. What is more, a fuller answer to such questions may be had only after considering that person on these particular occasions in comparison with others both similarly and differently circumstanced. For instance, a man in health is freer than the same man ill. Similarly, a man out of prison is freer than the same man in prison. Yet we might want to say that a man in failing health but not in prison is not as free as a man in good health in prison. It must be noticed, however, that any comparisons of freedoms will depend on what the person who makes the comparison holds to be most valuable. For instance, I have known adults who envy children their freedom, yet I have also known children who were envious of adults' freedom. It does seem possible to draw up a kind of yardstick against which different freedoms might be compared; but it would be more instructive for the reader to make his own yardstick and argue it out with his friends than for me to set out mine. For the relative values which such a yardstick expresses, and consequently its interest, depend on each person's beliefs about the freedoms that he and others ought to enjoy.

Talk about human freedom, then, makes sense when it is relative to a particular person's actions at a given time, and when that person is compared with others both similarly and differently situated. The level at which discussions are most profitable is that of questions like "Was X free when he did Y?" It may turn out that each time we have to answer a question like this, we must always say, "In this case X could not have done otherwise." Should this be so, while philosophy has shown us what the word "free" means, that is, while we know the sort of case to which it applies, if we never can find such a case, we shall never have occasion to say that anyone is free. It is not for philosophers to establish that there are human beings who are free. Their task is only to show that talk about human freedom is intelligible. It remains then for us to examine our own lives to see if there are times when we can say that we are free.

I now want to examine two claims that man is not free, which must be disposed of before we may feel secure in talking of human freedom. They are the claim that man cannot be free because his actions are governed by fate, and the claim that man cannot be free because his actions are causally determined.

## FATED OR FREE

The doctrine that fate is the cause of all human actions is sometimes stated as "Whatever you do or whatever happens to you, fate has decreed it." Or similarly, "Whatever is, God has willed it." Or take the closely related views: "When your time is up, the bullet with your name on it won't miss"; and "I landed on my feet, without a scratch. It just wasn't my turn."

Let us consider the decrees of fate, with the understanding that whatever is said about fate applies also to the will of God in this context. Sometimes when someone is told that fate has decreed that he must do whatever it is he is doing, he answers by saying that he is conscious of having chosen to act; and thus he is led to believe that he could have done otherwise; and if he could have done otherwise, how could he be fated to act as he did? The fatalist's reply is that fate has decreed that the person *choose* as he did. Fate dictates everything. Thus, any feelings of freedom which someone may have are illusory. There appears to be no escape from the domain of fate. But when all else fails, philosophy may show a way. We must ask what it means to say that fate governs all.

In order for me to know what it means to say that all my choices are governed by fate. I must know what it would be like to make a choice not governed by fate. Yet the fatalist leaves no room for even the possibility of such a condition to exist when choices are made. In order for me to tell that a certain action is governed by fate, I should be able to tell what it would be like for the action not to be governed by fate. But the fatalist denies the possibility of any such differentiation among actions. Even when I sometimes think that I might have done otherwise, he claims that my actions are nonetheless governed by fate. What greater difference could there be between fated actions and free?

Yet, according to the fatalist, this difference makes no difference. But if there is no difference, the claim that all my actions are governed by fate is meaningless. I may begin to worry over the fated character of my actions when the fatalist shows me how to tell the difference between my doing something because of fate and my just doing it. But so long as the fatalist claims that whatever I do is governed by fate and could not be otherwise, he makes a poor beginning on this task.

Indeed, for the fatalist to make his position intelligible is to defeat it. There are plenty of times when I may say that I could not have done otherwise. The robber's pistol. The unexpected guest. The plea of an old friend. The burned-out motor in the middle of the desert. The trip to the dentist. In these situations we learn what it is like not to be able to do otherwise; and thus we can imagine what it would be like, spending our whole lives not able to do otherwise. But notice that these "I could not have done otherwise" situations form a collection of their own only by contrast with situations in which I could have done otherwise. The contrast is what enables me to distinguish them. If my life really were one of not being able to do otherwise, if I had never known a different kind of life, or if I could never observe such a life in another, or if I could never imagine such a life, I should have no reason to regard my life as one in which I could not do otherwise. Yet this is just the sort of life which the fatalist wants us to understand that we do lead. The concept of fate takes its seeming sense from our knowledge of helpless and hopeless situations; but in claiming that all is helpless and hopeless, the fatalist legislates out of existence, even out of conceivability, the very situations whose contrast makes "helpless" and "hopeless" meaningful.

We may deal in a similar way with the "If they're gonna get me, they're gonna get me" class of remarks. Such observations are properly consoling to soldiers on the firing line and small boys walking past cemeteries in the dark. They have the merit of taking one's mind off one's fears and letting one attend to the business at hand. The philosophical interest in the "When your time comes" doctrine, however, is to be found in the question of knowing when it is your time. Unfortunately, one can never know that a given time is not his until the time is past. *His time* is identified by a test from which the tester can never profit. The philosopher may agree that while the occasional emotional value of the doctrine is great, its value as a long-term guide in life is nil.

## CAUSATION, DETERMINISM, AND FREEDOM

I now want to examine the bogey of causal determinism. The bogey arises when one regards the world as an orderly system in which chains of causes and effects are discoverable, and then agrees to the universal applicability of the dictum, "Every event has a cause." But if every event has a cause, then what I am doing right now has been caused by what has immediately preceded it; and that set of events has in turn been caused by a set of preceding events. Now this is the point at which the bogey may spring upon us. Frightened people say, "Well, if everything is caused by what has gone before, then it had to be as it is. Then nothing could have been otherwise and everything is determined, even human action; and there is no such thing as human freedom. How then can anyone help doing whatever he is doing right now?"

Before we succumb to the terrors of determinism, however, it would be well to consider carefully the respect in which the dictum, "Every event has a cause," is applicable to human actions. As a beginning we may go a long way toward reducing determinism's impressiveness by noticing how little the dictum says. It means no more than that in principle a cause can be found for every event. It does not claim that a particular kind of event must always be the result of the same kind of cause, although we are, of course, inclined to expect such a relationship to hold. Nor does it claim that a certain kind of thing must always be the cause of the same kind of event, although we are, of course, inclined to expect such a relationship to hold. Anyone who claims that these relationships hold in some absolute and incontrovertible sense assumes more than experience warrants. "Every event has a cause" must not be understood then as the assertion that we live in a world of unfailing causal connections. The negation of every statement about causes and effects is conceivable. This consideration alone goes far toward establishing the possibility of human freedom, for from it we may argue that in any instance of human action, it is at least conceivable that the person might have done otherwise.

But what is meant here by "human action"? Consider the following examples drawn from western movies. Tom knocks a gun out of Dick's hand because Harry bumped into Tom and Tom was bumped against Dick. Now contrast this example with the following one: Tom strikes Dick's hand with his own hand and knocks Dick's gun to the floor. I mean these examples to illustrate in a rough way the following distinctions. What Tom does in the second example is a human action; but Tom's part in the first example is not a human action. Notice, however, that what happens in both examples could be described by the same sentence: "Tom knocked Dick's gun out of his hand." But to say no more would be to conceal a distinction of the greatest importance. For in the first example Harry is the cause of Tom's knocking Dick's gun out of his hand (speaking, I think, carelessly, we might ordinarily say that Harry is the cause of *Tom's action*), and in the second example Tom is himself the cause of the gun's being knocked to the floor. But what is meant by "Tom is himself the cause"? To answer this question, consider what Tom might say in each example if we asked why he knocked Dick's gun out of his hand. In the first example he would say, "Harry bumped me," that is, he gives the cause of what happened. In the second example he might say, "I wanted to get the gun out of Dick's hand," that is, he gives the reason for his action; he states what he intended to accomplish. Of course, if Tom says, "I was hypnotized," or, "Harry was holding a gun on me and he ordered me to do it," then he is not giving the reason for his action but telling the cause of it.

This distinction between a person's giving a reason and naming a cause provides the basis for our distinction between actions in the sense of a person's self-originated actions and all other oc-

currences which may be called a person's actions but are so only
in a loose sense of the word. We must now connect this notion
of self-originated human action with our earlier account of human freedom as any occasion on which someone could have
acted otherwise. The connection is simply that part of what is
meant by saying that someone acted for a reason is that he could
have acted in some other way had he reason to do so. Occasions
on which a person acts for a reason are then prime instances
of occasions on which he could have done otherwise.

If we turn now to the question of applying the dictum, "Every
event has a cause," to human actions, I believe that we have some
clues as to how to proceed. We may begin by enunciating a
tautology which the determinist neglects: Men are men and not
billiard balls. The force of this truism is that not everything
said to be done by a person can be accounted for as a reaction to
an external force as one can account for the behavior of a billiard
ball by citing the thrust of the cue, the state of the cloth, and
so on. There are human actions whose explanation requires citing a reason. Now if we say of such actions that they too are
covered by the dictum, "Every event has a cause," we must be
very careful to notice what the word "cause" means here. It means
that someone had a reason for what he did, and thus it is he
who is responsible for his action. But if it is he who is responsible,
then he was not made to act as he did by an external force as
the determinist claims. Thus, even though we apply the dictum,
"Every event has a cause," to human actions, we escape the bogey
of determinism.

The determinist may rally at this point and reply that it is
true that there may be persons who sometimes act for reasons,
and on these occasions we may say that they are free, but nonetheless they were made to be the kind of person they are. So determinism is true after all. But if this is the sense in which determinism is true, it means no more than that every event has a
cause; and this we have never denied. When we say that the
congenital idiot's heredity is the cause of his *lack* of freedom,
and that the stone walls which surround the prisoner are the
cause of his lack of freedom, why should we want to claim that

in order for freedom to exist it must be the one thing that is uncaused? We must not lose sight of the fact that a person's freedom depends not on the origin of his being able to act for reasons, but on his actually being able to do so.

The determinist has a last string to his bow which it would be just as well to break before we leave this topic. He argues that if we allow that "Every event has a cause" is applicable to human action, then we make human actions predictable; and predictable actions are not free actions. We may reply that it is true that, if I know that Tom has a reason for acting in a certain way, I can predict that given a situation in which this kind of action fits, Tom will act as he has reason to do. But does my knowledge that Tom has reason to act in a certain way lessen his freedom to act in that way? I think not. For if my knowing how Tom might act will lessen his freedom, so must Tom's own knowledge of how he will act. But it would be absurd to claim that with such knowledge his freedom is removed, because without it he could not act at all. But if Tom's own ability to predict how he is going to act in no way affects his freedom, how could my being able to do so affect it? Once more we find the determinist pressing for more than the facts warrant.

## "Freedom of the Will"

Throughout this discussion of human freedom, I have avoided talking about "the will," a concept long cherished by philosophers. It would be unfair to those readers who have trusted me to introduce them to philosophy if I said nothing about this philosophers' darling. So I shall, by way of explaining why I have avoided it. Our having wills was postulated by those philosophers who thought it necessary to endow human beings with a special mental organ that might serve as an uncaused cause of human action, and hence guarantee human freedom. But we are released from the task of fathoming the occult operations of human wills as soon as we see that a consideration of what it is to be a person provides a way of accounting for human freedom, and solves the problems that were meant to be solved by postulating the existence of the will. The wisdom of this course may be seen in two different developments. First, instead of talking about this mysterious organ the will, some philosophers have turned to the task of elucidating what is meant when someone says, "I will . . ." "I have decided that . . ." "I promise . . ." "I choose . . ." "X is weak-willed," and similar expressions. Second, nowadays, while many philosophers who wish to discuss human freedom announce their topic as "Freedom of the Will," they confine themselves to elucidating the concept of "freedom" with never a word about the will. In short, they mention "the will" for old times' sake; but they know that their business lies elsewhere. Hence, I have relegated "the will" to this historical note, and kept that source of confusion out of my discussion of human freedom.

### SUGGESTIONS FOR FURTHER READING

The topics discussed in this chapter are the most abstruse in philosophy. In two recent studies their authors have the advantage of book-length areas of maneuver; but they still demand close attention from the reader. These books are *The Freedom of the Will* by Austin M. Farrer (A. and C. Black, London, 1958) and *Thought and Action* by Stuart Hampshire (Viking, New York, 1960). A general survey of mental acts (of which willing is one variety) which may be especially recommended is *Concept of Mind* by Gilbert Ryle (Barnes and Noble).

## SIX

Three different accounts of the basis for the moral order are examined in this chapter. The following books are suggested for joint reading: For the Idea of the Good, *Republic* by Plato; for nature, *Nicomachean Ethics* by Aristotle and the essay "Nature" in *Nature and Utility of Religion* by John Stuart Mill (Liberal Arts); for moral sentiments, *Hume's Moral and Political Philosophy* edited by H. D. Aiken (Hafner), which contains the moral philosophy from *A Treatise of Human Nature* and all of *An Enquiry Concerning the Principles of Morals.*

# Philosophy and Morals

In this chapter I shall consider what some philosophers have had to say about morality. They have not all thought that the same sort of thing could be said; and we shall have to examine not only what certain philosophers have said, and why they have said it, but also why other philosophers have thought that what they have said should not be said. In reading this chapter one should remember that morality at its edges runs into the allied domains of law, etiquette, courtesy, manners, custom, and politics. In this chapter I shall not have room to say anything of these alliances, beyond this reminder of their existence. In the next chapter, Philosophy and Politics, I shall discuss one of morality's near relations; and that chapter may be regarded as a necessary continuation of this one.

## MORAL RULES AND MORAL JUDGMENTS

Morality has to do with making and following rules that are intended to govern human actions. It presupposes that men are free to act in one way rather than another; and it presupposes that men may reflect on the way they act, and that some means other than force can be found to convince them to act in a given way rather than in any other. Moral rules are easier to exemplify than to define. Certain of the Ten Commandments are good examples:

Thou shalt not kill.
Thou shalt not steal.
Thou shalt not bear false witness against thy neighbor.

Why may these commandments be said to be moral rules? They are rules for someone's getting along with other people; and it is generally agreed that such rules are moral rules. But perhaps not just any rule for getting along with others should be counted as a moral rule. Probably only the more important of these rules should be so counted; but the criterion of importance is not easy to determine, for different people might place more emphasis on one rule than another. I believe that the rule, "Thou shalt not kill," is more important than "Guard against halitosis"; and I count only the former as a moral rule, although both have to do with getting along with others. Nonetheless, I can imagine someone who might value sweet-smelling murderers over more peaceable persons who fail to brush their teeth after every meal.

As well as saying that morality has to do with getting along with others, there are philosophers who want morality to include a person's getting along with himself, or as it is sometimes put, a person's fulfilling his duties to himself. What is it like to have a duty to oneself? The possibility of self-neglect, or more dramatically, suicide, suggested to Kant, for example, that there must be duties to oneself. He thought that either committing suicide, or, less violently, simply failing to improve oneself by developing and exercising one's talents were both ways in which someone could be untrue to himself, and that someone who behaved in these ways resembles a person who fails in his obligations to others. Hence, Kant thought that morality extended to a person's regard for himself; so there could be moral rules on the order of "Preserve your life," and "Develop your talents." Similarly, Socrates regularly advised, "Know thyself."

Closely related to moral rules is another kind of moral sentence: moral judgments. Here are some sample moral judgments:

Killing is wicked.
Stealing is wrong.
Fathers do the right thing when they endeavor to correct their children's misbehavior.

In each of these statements there is a value word: wicked, wrong, right. These are some of the commonest value words that have a moral flavor. Others are good, bad, nice, fine, grand, noble, admirable, virtuous, naughty, nasty, abominable, and vicious. When we find one of these words applied to an action, its presence usually marks the sentence as a moral judgment. One of the tasks of moral philosophy is to describe the ways in which we use these words, working out their contexts and interrelations. In this chapter, I shall be able to do no more than say something about one of these words: "good," largely because it is the one on which moral philosophers have spent most of their time.

I have said that moral rules and moral judgments are closely related; but what is their relationship? One of their relations must be that they imply one another; that is, if you agree with a certain moral judgment then you must agree to follow the moral rule that may be derived from it, or if you agree that a certain moral rule must be followed, then you must agree with the moral judgment on which it is based. How does it come about that moral rules and moral judgments imply one another? At least one of the uses which we have for value words is to express approval (or disapproval) and, hence, to encourage (or discourage) action. "Good," for example, may be used to express approval and to encourage action; and "bad" may be used to express disapproval and to discourage action. So when I say, "Stealing is a bad thing to do," I am saying, at least, that I disapprove of stealing, and hence that I wish to discourage others from stealing; so my judgment implies the moral rule, "Do not steal." When I say, "Do not steal," and I am understood to be announcing or repeating a moral rule, then it follows that the above imperative implies such moral judgments as "Stealing is a bad thing to do," and "People who do not steal are good." For someone to affirm a moral judgment but to deny the rule it implies, or to repeat the rule but to deny the judgment is for him to contradict himself. Which comes first, moral rules or moral judgment? Judgments must have a logical priority over rules for it is to them that we must appeal in order to justify our teaching and following the rules.

A moral man, then, is someone who is following a set of moral rules, a moral code. Where does he get his rules? He gets them from a moralist, that is, from someone who is skilled in making moral judgments and in pointing out the rules that follow from them. (It is possible, of course, for a person to be his own moralist; and it is one of the consequences of the Reformation that "Each man his own moralist" is an ideal of Protestant societies. Hume's moral philosophy, which is examined later in this chapter, is an expression of this ideal.) Given, then, our moral man following the rules which the moralist has taught him, we may then ask the philosopher's question: "Is the moral man following the *right* moral code?" Here we meet the following problem in the hierarchy of justification. Moral rules are justified by moral judgments, but how are moral judgments justified? As an illustration of the hierarchy of justification, let us consider the commandment, "Thou shalt not kill," which I offered earlier as an example of a moral rule. Since the rule is a divine command, the statement of the moral judgment, "Killing is wicked," is an unnecessary step in its justification; but to give our example the usual pattern, it may be inserted here, and then we may ask, "How did Moses, the moralist, know that killing is wicked?" The answer is that he knew that for one man to murder another is to act against God's will. God's will is the ultimate justification for the moral rules which Moses propounded. But what is meant by "ultimate justification" here? The justification of any of Moses' rules by an appeal to God's will is ultimate in the sense that for Moses no further questions about the *rightness* of the rules was appropriate. There is no room for argument with God.

The Ten Commandments and their justification may serve us both as an example of the way moral rules are justified and as an illustration of the connection between a moral code and a religion. Any moralist who speaks within a religious context will attempt to justify the moral rules he advocates in the way that has just been described. In this chapter, however, I want to consider the question of the rightness of moral rules outside the context of a religion. To consider morals in relation to religion finally leads one to the question of which religion one should believe in, a question which I have already carried as far as it is fitting for me to do in Chapter 4. Therefore I can most profitably confine myself to a consideration of extra-religious guarantees of moral judgments. These have commanded the attention of the greater number of moral philosophers for two reasons, both historical. In the first place, the religion of the ancient Greeks who invented philosophy did not claim dominion over all departments of human intelligence and endeavor. Hence, these philosophers were free to seek extra-religious justification for morality. In the second place, since the seventeenth century, philosophers have felt free to look for extra-religious solutions to the problem of guaranteeing moral judgments, either because they had no religious beliefs to restrict their inquiries, or because they thought religious beliefs themselves stand in need of some sort of extra-religious justification.

Moral philosophers have approached the problem of justifying the moralist's judgments in two different ways. The earlier approach is characterized by the belief that there is some special object of knowledge with which the moralist is acquainted; and it is his acquaintance with this object which guarantees the moral judgments which he makes. The later approach grew out of doubts about the existence of any special object of moral knowledge. Of the nature of these doubts I shall have more to say later; but from them springs the view that the origin of the moral order is to be found in man himself, so that the moralist himself, in a way which I shall presently describe, guarantees his views of man's nature and duties. Plato and Aristotle are two of the most famous proponents of the view that there is a moral order existing independently of man and waiting to be discovered by him, although they differ sharply about the character of this moral order. Hume is one of the most famous proponents of the view that the moral order originates in man. It is the views of these philosophers which I shall now examine in turn.

## MORAL ORDER AND WORLD ORDER: PLATO

Plato thought, at least for a time, that the meaning of words might be accounted for by supposing that their prime meaning is an Idea (ideal form); and that we might know that we are using a word correctly when we can tell that the object to which we apply the word resembles the Idea which the word names. Plato was particularly interested in the word "good." Its meaning can be of the greatest importance in the statement of moral judgments; and Plato thought that the moralist's work could be put on a sound basis if he were able, as he made his moral judgments, to use the word "good" with a knowledge of the Idea of the Good. Plato's answer, then, to the question of what can guarantee the rightness of the moralist's judgments is the Idea of the Good; and it is this contention which I now wish to consider.

In my discussion of philosophy and the world, I have already examined the plausibility of Plato's claim that a world of Ideas exists above the world of sense; and I have argued that for various reasons it is doubtful that these claims can be substantiated. But here let the existence of Ideas be granted, and let us ask if there is any way in which a moralist's knowledge of the Idea of the Good will guarantee his judgments. If a moralist could know the Good, then it is to be supposed that his conception of the good man and his duties would be shaped in accordance with the Idea of the Good. But immediately we are faced with a curious difficulty in Plato's moral philosophy. It is that no one but the moralist could know whether the Idea of the Good is guaranteeing his work. This difficulty arises from another difficulty: that of knowing the Idea of the Good. I do not mean here the logical and empirical difficulties in the way of knowing any Idea, which Plato's critics find it easy to raise. I mean rather the obstacles which Plato himself recognizes. To know the Idea of the Good requires a long and arduous training, involving a series of trials which only a few candidates succeed in surviving. Indeed, it would seem that so few can, that the moralist's task necessarily devolves on them. Therefore there is no possibility of there being an independent moral philosopher, someone not engaged in the immediate task of announcing moral judgments, who can check on whether the judgments made by the few moralists are a reflection of the Idea of the Good. What is more, there is no chance for ordinary people to check on the moralist's work. By their ignorance they are forever bound to take the moralist's word for the rightness of his pronouncements. This would mean that in principle ordinary people could never be moral in an enlightened sense, but only in an "obedient dog" sense. Indeed, the consequence of Plato's moral philosophy is that people might be moral without knowing that they are being moral. Now I should like to challenge this consequence by an appeal to what we ordinarily understand by morality. I ask the reader to consider for himself this question: Even though someone had acted in a way that we would ordinarily say is moral, if this person did not know that his action was moral, would we say that he had acted morally? I believe that the answer to this question is "No." We ordinarily give moral credit for conscientiousness and not chance. So far as I can see, then, this curious difficulty in Plato's moral philosophy, the exclusiveness of the moralist's knowledge of the foundations of morals, is insurmountable.

But let us suppose that not only moralists, but quite ordinary people, could know the Idea of the Good; and let us suppose that it is possible for everyone to see that the moralist's conception of the good man and his duties is a reflection of the Idea of the Good; that is, everyone can see that the moralist's judgments follow from the Idea of the Good. Now, even supposing all of these possibilities, some moral philosophers have doubted that a knowledge of the Good, and a knowledge of the judgments and rules derivable from that Idea, are sufficient to make men moral. The difficulty may be stated in this way: It is conceivable that someone might say, "So, I know the Good; but why should I be good?" It is unsatisfactory to say to such a person, "But you *ought* to want to imitate the Good," for he may still ask, "But why ought I to want to imitate the Good?" And it is no use saying, "Because it is the Good, you idiot!" For he does *know* that; but he does not *feel* bound to imitate the Good. The possibility, then, of this divorce between knowledge and inclination makes it extremely doubtful that a knowledge of the Idea of the Good could by itself bring people to be moral.

## WORLD ORDER AND MORAL ORDER: ARISTOTLE

Aristotle was no less interested than his teacher Plato in the question of how the rightness of the moralist's pronouncements can be guaranteed. But, as I noticed in my discussion of philosophy and the world, Aristotle found so many difficulties in Plato's theory of Ideas that he despaired of ever making sense of Plato's claim that there is a world of Ideas superior to the world of sense experience. Thus, when he turned to moral philosophy, he had little use for Plato's claim that there is a moral order above the world order which provides the foundation for morality in this world. Indeed, he by-passes questions about the relation of a transcendent moral order to the world order by arguing that the world order is the moral order. To state Aristotle's moral philosophy in a sentence: The natural is the good. The guarantee of the moralist's pronouncements is nature; and to discover the rightness of what the moralist says, we need only to ask of his rules, "Does he enjoin us to do the natural?" or to ask of his judgments, "Has he decided in accordance with nature?"

Aristotle supports his moral philosophy with a concept taken from his view of the world, the concept of the nature of a thing. Everything has an end which it seeks to accomplish; and we know the nature of a thing when we discover the end it is seeking to accomplish. To illustrate Aristotle's view of the connection between the natural and the moral, let us consider his view of man's moral duty as discovered by considering his nature. The clue to what something's end is, is to notice how its *kind* of thing differs from every other kind of thing. Then its end is to develop as far as possible along the lines indicated by this difference.

When Aristotle considers man, he finds that man differs from everything else in the possession of intelligence (the power to acquire knowledge). Therefore he argues that the end of man is the exercise of his intelligence, and the excellence of a man is to be judged by the amount he knows. Aristotle knows that many people would say that the goal of men is to be happy. But he is also aware of the fact that "happy" is a word which can be used in many different ways. What he wants to know, then, is whether there is any way of specifying what human happiness must be, so that men may intelligently pursue this goal; and he believes that the question can be answered in this way: A man's happiness lies in his fulfilling his nature, i.e. the exercise of his intelligence. Now Aristotle does not deny that man may find pleasure in many things: wine, women, and song, for example. But if happiness means enduring and unstinted pleasure, then, for Aristotle, it can only be found in what we may call the life of the mind; and this is man's true happiness, because it is most in conformity with his nature.

This account of Aristotle's moral philosophy mentions only his advocacy of intellectual virtue. In fairness to Aristotle, I must point out that he has much to say of the social virtues, such as courage, honesty, and friendship. But while he regards man's life in society as worthy of his attention, it is clear that he regards a life devoted solely to social duties as less valuable than one devoted to the exercise of intelligence in the pursuit of knowledge. Spending time in either politics or war is all very well for those who are capable of nothing better; but engaging in these activities is not the best life for a man capable of the pursuit of knowledge, for this is the highest activity of which man's nature is capable.

Now what can be said for Aristotle's solution to the problems of moral philosophy: The natural is the moral? I am afraid that Aristotle's views suffer from one enormous difficulty at the very outset: How is one to determine what the natural is? I have said that Aristotle answers this question by saying that the end or goal of a certain kind of thing distinguishes it from all other

things, so that what is natural for something is whatever it must
do to fulfill its end. But what reply could Aristotle make to some
bloodthirsty general who might use his principles in the following way: It is true that man is remarkable among all other crea-
tures for his intelligence, but man is also remarkably capable
of making war; so man's capacity to make war, a capacity which
he exhibits to a greater degree than any other creature, indicates
that his end is to shed blood. Therefore the natural, and consequently the moral, man is the warrior. What is more, it seems
not impossible that similar arguments might be advanced by the
lecher, the robber, the wastrel, and the indolent, to mention only
a few of those who might make an alarming use of Aristotle's
doctrine that the natural is the moral.

I believe that the above argument, which seems to me un-
answerable, must persuade us that Aristotle must have had some
criterion for what is natural in man other than the one he states.
I believe that in giving his account of what he believed to be
natural in man, Aristotle was really citing what he admired most
in man. Indeed, he was really describing his own mode of life.
For we must remember that later ages have given him the title,
"The Master of Those Who Know," in tribute to the range of
his knowledge. If I am right about Aristotle, then he confused
the admirable with the natural, and endeavored to justify his
own way of life with the claim that it was natural to man, and
the natural is the moral.

There is yet another objection which may be made to Aristotle's
moral philosophy; and we have already seen the force of a similar
objection to Plato's use of the Idea of the Good. It is that it does
seem possible for someone to agree that whatever is natural is
good, and he might agree that certain ways of acting are natural,
but even though he might have this knowledge, he need not feel
compelled to act in ways that are said to be natural, and therefore moral. Thus, Aristotle's moral philosophy also appears to be
snagged on the problem of connecting moral knowledge and
moral action.

## THE MORAL ORDER WITHIN: HUME

Moral philosophy for Hume is not the same enterprise it is for Plato and Aristotle. The change can be briefly characterized by saying that Plato and Aristotle are interested in finding the answer to the question, "What is the good?" while Hume is interested in the question, "What does the moralist mean when he says that something is good?" It may be thought that these two questions are alike, but that they are not is shown by the difference in their answers. Plato and Aristotle thought that their question could be answered by engaging in a search to discover what the good is; and each found an answer. Plato: The good is the Idea of the Good. Aristotle: The good is the natural. But Hume's question turns out to be a question about the psychology of the moralist. We shall know what the good is when we know why the moralist says that certain actions are good; and, put in a single sentence, Hume's answer is that the moralist calls certain actions good because they please him. Or to put the difference between Hume and Plato and Aristotle in another way, Hume does not believe that it is his business to provide morality with foundations. He is merely exhibiting the foundations which it has.

Hume believes that when we say that an action is good, we mean that it pleases us; and correspondingly, when we say that an action is bad, we mean that it displeases us. He argues for his views in this way:

Take any action allow'd to be vicious: Wilful murder, for instance . . . The vice entirely escapes you, as long as you consider the object. You never can find it, till you turn your reflexion into your own breast, and find a sentiment of disapprobation, which arises in you, towards this action. Here is a matter of fact; but 'tis the object of feeling, not of reason. It lies in yourself, not in the object. So that when you pronounce any action or character to be vicious, you mean nothing, but that from the constitution of your nature you have a feeling or sentiment of blame from the contemplation of it. . . . Nothing can be more real, or concern us more, than our own sentiments of pleasure and uneasiness; and if these be favourable to virtue, and unfavourable to vice, no more can be requisite to the regulation of our conduct and behaviour.[1]

An action may be pleasing for either one of two reasons: It may be pleasing in itself or it may be pleasing as a means to something else. I might find benevolence, for example, pleasing in itself; but to carry the illustration to the limit, let us suppose that I find benevolence pleasing as a means to something else. Now in the hierarchy, or order, of things that are pleasing as a means to other things, there must be at least one thing which is ultimately pleasing in itself, or the order of things pleasing as means to something else would be endless. The thing which Hume regards as complex enough for many human actions to be means to it, and therefore great enough to be a notable end in itself is the maintenance of society or social harmony.

Why does Hume claim that my acting morally depends on the pleasure I find in moral action and my avoiding immoral actions depends on my desire to avoid uneasiness? This claim is his answer to a question which we have already noticed that the moral philosophies of Plato and Aristotle leave unanswered: How are we to close the gap between knowing the good and doing the good? Hume's point is that it is my being pleased by benevolence and by social harmony that gives them their moral importance. Without my pleasure, I might see that benevolence contributes to social harmony, but neither benevolence nor social harmony would be of any moral interest to me, and social harmony would never be a moral end in itself for me. Thus, Hume believes that in the pleasure we take in certain ways of acting, he has exhibited the foundations of morality.

We must be careful to see just what sort of foundation Hume discovers morality to have. Notice that he does not speak as a moralist and concern himself about what ought to please people, nor does he consider whether there ought to be anything that pleases everyone. He does believe that, as a matter of fact, everyone is pleased by social harmony, and pleased because it is advantageous to live in a harmonious society. But he does not appear as the advocate of either social harmony or the pursuit of

[1] David Hume, *A Treatise of Human Nature,* Bk. III, "Of Morals," Pt. I, Sect. I.

advantage. Rather he seeks to show why these things can have something to do with morality. His moral philosophy leaves open the question of whether there is, or ought to be, a single morality, and merely claims that whatever actions or goals are counted as moral will be so because they please. Hume has shown then how to find out what may be regarded as good; but he is not committed to any one answer to the question of what is the good, for he believes that for different people there may be many different goods. In his writings Hume reveals his characteristically eighteenth-century allegiance to the ideal of social harmony. But he also exhibits that peculiarly eighteenth-century combination of a knowledge of the fact that in different places men exhibit different manners and a belief in the universal reasonableness of men. Hence, social harmony is a vague ideal which might be achieved by several sorts of social arrangements. But it is clear that while, for Hume, a moral philosopher never specifies what is the good, a moralist, to make moral judgments, must have a steady view of what is the good. All Hume claims to have done is to have given an account of why the moralist judges as he does.

But now what can we say when we come to the question of whether what Hume says is of any use in discovering the rightness of a moralist's judgments? Clearly, if I am to be in any position to evaluate a moralist's judgments, I must like what he likes, and above all I must be pleased with that which ultimately pleases him. But see the curious conclusion to which we are now led. If I like what the moralist likes, how can I help but agree with the rightness of his moral judgments? But if I disagree with what he likes, while I may understand why he judges as he does, I will certainly regard his judgments as wrong. Now where does this leave us? The moralist's task turns out to be not only telling people what is good, but persuading them to like the good. Persuading and not forcing, because forcing means revolt as soon as the force is removed. The moralist's task then is not one of argument, but of seizing on or creating situations from which the moral point may be drawn for those who experience the situation. Indeed, much of his persuasion may have to be left until someone has made a moral mistake, for it may not be until then that the moral point may be seen; and even then there will be pupils who will miss it. In short, "I like it" is a perfectly respectable moral defense for any action; but the world is as good as it is because the moralist is able to reply, "Yes. But there is something I want you to like more."

We may now turn to the question of whether Hume has given a satisfactory account of the foundations of morality. We may assess what he says by trying it against two bogeys which regularly haunt moral philosophy, the conflict between objectivism and subjectivism, and the tension between absolutism and relativism.

Hume argues that the moralist calls good those things which please him. Hence, the moralist's judgments, his approval and disapproval of certain ways of acting, and his prescription of appropriate moral rules are all to be traced back to his being pleased. On this account of the moralist's views, they are based on his own feelings and thus may be said to be subjective. Opposed to the subjectivist is the objectivist who desires some foundation for morality independent of human determination. Let us see what an argument between an objectivist moral philosopher and a Humean might be like.

*Objectivist:* Let us suppose that there is a moralist who says that one man's taking the life of another is a bad thing. Now why do you suppose that he might say that?

*Humean:* The moralist might believe that man should be a preserver of life. This view is part of his conception of the ideal man. Since killing goes against this ideal, he counts it as a bad action.

*Objectivist:* All right. But why is being a preserver of life part of the moralist's conception of the ideal man?

*Humean:* He probably prefers to live with that kind of person.

*Objectivist:* And so should I. But I am disturbed by your accounting for the moralist's ideal by saying that he likes it. For I do not see what reply he could make to someone who says, "I like another conception of man, the man who gets what he wants even if he has to kill for it. Killing is a good thing when it enables a man to get what he wants."

*Humean:* I believe that the moralist would say first that his liking the conception of man as a preserver of life hinges on another and superior ideal, a peaceful society. His liking social harmony explains his liking the man who respects human life.

*Objectivist:* Once again I must say that I agree with this moralist's likes, but I am distressed by his supporting his moral ideal with no more than his liking it. For my earlier objection still pursues him. What could he say to someone who dislikes social harmony, indeed who likes asocial chaos and seizes every means to promote it? Such a person judges that murder is a good thing. Our moralist judges that it is a bad thing. Each of them bases his judgment on an ideal that each likes. How could either one of them say that the other is wrong? Or how could a third person tell which of them is right? Likes seem to me to prove nothing, and this is why I ask for some guarantee of moral judgments which is objective, that is independent of anyone's likes or dislikes. This sort of guarantee appears to me to be the only sort that can be agreed on. The Idea of the Good may be unknowable. Appeals to nature may be unworkable. But surely we can find some objective guarantee of morality. Something which shows more promise as grounds for agreement than an appeal to the emotions.

*Humean:* But your question is not so much about the foundation of morals as it is about whether moral argeement could be achieved. I take it that you would have no objection to a moral philosopher's saying that the ultimate basis of moral ideals is feeling, if you could infer from a harmony of opinions that everyone feels alike on moral matters. Now if what you are bothered about is the existence of moral disagreement, I assure you that it will be removed when everyone feels alike. There is nothing inherent in feeling to prevent its providing a universal basis for morality. But please do not misunderstand me. I do not mean to claim that everyone does now agree in moral feelings. I only mean to show that my subjective account of the foundations of morality is not defeated by showing that a feeling for some particular morality is not universal in mankind.

*Objectivist:* Let me try firing at you from a different direction. It seems curious to say that the basis of the morality which a moralist advocates is his feelings, for most moralists do not cite their own feelings as the guarantee of their moral judgments. Take for instance a religious moralist who cites the will of God as the guarantee of his moral judgments.

*Humean:* It looks as though I should have to say that there are many moralists who do not completely understand their business. Their feelings might very well be their moral guides without their noticing it. After all, if a moralist tells me that I should do something because it is God's will, will I do it if I do not value doing God's will above everything else? What is more, his ultimate defense of the morality which he advocates is surely that he himself values the doing of God's will above everything else.

*Objectivist:* The other questions which follow on here may appropriately be asked by my cousin, the Absolutist, for our interests run together at this point.

*Absolutist:* I have been following your conversation with Objectivist, and I want to begin by raising a difficulty of my own. You do not seem worried that, when feelings of liking and disliking are the basis of morality, morality becomes relative to the feelings of a given moralist. I should like a morality which transcends all moralists and is absolute and invariable throughout mankind; and I do not see that the account of the foundations of morality which you offer could assure me of the possibility of the universal morality I seek.

*Humean:* Well, Absolutist, I must tell you in a slightly different way what I have already said to Objectivist. I do not believe that you would have any complaint about feelings as the basis of morality if all moralists felt alike; and I need not be unsympathetic to your desire for a universality of moral opinion, in order to defend my account of the foundations of morality. The fact that feeling is the basis of morality in no way makes a universal morality impossible. For those who desire it, their task is clear. They must persuade everyone to have the same moral feelings. Not an easy task surely, but no more difficult than persuading everyone to accept some belief as the basis of morality. And I ask you, could they accept such a belief, if they did not like accepting it and were free to reject it?

*Absolutist:* You say that it is a fact that feelings are the basis of morality. Could this claim ever be false?

*Humean:* Since it is a fact, it could certainly be false; and I stand ready to examine any considerations which might show it to be false. But other than saying that these considerations must be an account of some basis for morality other than being pleased and displeased, I cannot say what they would be. To expect more would be like asking me to tell you what the world would be like without the force of gravity. I really couldn't say, beyond saying that there would be no gravity, because our conception of what the world must be like is so closely tied to our understanding of the force of gravity.

*Absolutist:* The next question which occurs to me is that if it is true that feelings are the basis of morality, can "Ought I to like what the moralist likes?" have a negative answer?

*Humean:* Let us see what this question might mean. Suppose a moralist said, "You ought to obey the traffic lights." Why? "Your following them, along with everyone else, makes for a freer flow of traffic." So what? "A freer flow of traffic is to your advantage in getting you safely and easily where you want to go. You cannot argue against your own advantage, can you?"

Now, when someone says, "Ought I to like what the moralist likes?" it is similar to asking, "Ought I to pursue my own advantage?" My own advantage, in the long run, and taking into account the kind of world I want to live in. Now it is not inconceivable that someone might insist on doing what is not to his own advantage. I do not mean the loyalist who refuses to divulge the secret even at the expense of his life. I mean the sick man who refuses to take his medicine. Or the even sicker man who refuses to acknowledge the rights of others. Such people are beyond the reach of the moralist, in the first place. They are in no position to ask, "Ought I to feel as the moralist wants me to?" But when someone who is not sick in the senses I have described asks, "Ought I to feel as the moralist wants me to?" and when he sees the concurrence of morality and advantage, how could he not feel as the moralist directs? He could hold out against the moralist only when he sees a divergence of morality and advantage. What other sign is there of a false moralist?

*Absolutist:* Well, now, which is more important to morality, advantage or feeling?

*Humean:* Advantage is nothing without my feeling that it is an advantage. If my likes do not coincide with those of the moralist, how can he advise me? If I differ with him, he can persuade me to agree with him if he can convince me that I am mistaken about what is to my advantage. But what is he doing but showing me that I ought to like one way of life rather than another? Besides, it ought to be recognized that the more experience I have of life, the better able I am to consult my own advantage and, hence, the closer I am to being my own moralist.

*Absolutist:* Now I want to bring up something which is thought to be an important weapon in the criticism of moral philosophies and I think that I can bang away at you with it. I think that in your moral philosophy you commit the naturalistic fallacy. That is, you identify good with some feature of the world, when you should see that good is itself and not another thing. The naturalistic fallacy occurs in your philosophy in the following way. You would have a moralist say that what pleases him, social harmony, for example, is good, so that you appear to equate that which pleases the moralist with the good. That you are mistaken in doing so is shown by my being able to ask the question, "And is that which pleases the moralist good?" Now if "that which pleases the moralist" is the meaning of "good" this last question means no more than "Is that which pleases the moralist that which pleases the moralist?" which is certainly not what we intended to ask. This shows that the good cannot be defined by any other thing, and must be itself.

*Humean:* I am not at all sure that my moral philosophy contains the naturalistic fallacy. Let me remind you, first of all, that hunts for instances of the naturalistic fallacy are usually started by philosophers who want to show that good exists in the world as an irreducible entity whose status is peculiar to itself. But if good does have the status which these philosophers ascribe to it, it is curious that it cannot be shown by some more direct means than hunting for the naturalistic fallacy in moral philosophies.

My next point is a linguistic one. It seems to me that we ought to notice the difference between the good, a good, and the use of "good" as an adjective. I have never claimed that there is some particular stuff which is the good. The only way in which I can understand the phrase "the good" is to suppose that the person who uses it is talking about what is to him the most valuable thing in the world, that thing which pleases him most for itself. Similarly, when someone says that he finds something to be a good, I suppose that he may be shown to mean that it pleases him. So the good or goods might be all sorts of things, so long as they please. As for the use of "good" as an adjective, when something is said to be a good thing, I suppose that it is either pleasing in itself or it has some quality which makes it useful in acquiring another thing which is pleasing in itself.

With these remarks in mind, let us look at the moralist's statement that since social harmony pleases him as an end in itself it is a good; and let us suppose that the following argument is advanced: Can it be that social harmony is a good because it pleases the moralist? For we may ask, "Is that which pleases the moralist good?" and if "good" means "that which pleases the moralist" we are asking no more than "Is that which pleases the moralist that which pleases the moralist?" and this is a silly sounding question which we did not mean to ask; so while social harmony may be a good, it cannot be so because it pleases the moralist.

In reply to this argument, I should say that there is an understandable use for the question, "Is that which pleases the moralist good?" I might ask this question if I opened shop as a moralist evaluator. If I am pleased by, and thus value highly, moralists who advocate social harmony, I should certainly

count it as a good when I find a moralist who is pleased by
social harmony. Thus, it seems to me that if someone hunting
for the naturalistic fallacy believes that he has found it in my
moral philosophy, he is making a mistake. He has failed to
notice the level at which his question may be asked. Since there is
a level at which the question, "Is that which pleases the moralist
good?" can be asked in my moral philosophy, that is, at the
level of evaluating moralists, I do not believe that my moral
philosophy contains the naturalistic fallacy.

*Absolutist:* I think you must allow me one last comment on your
account of morality. Like my cousin, the Objectivist, I had
always supposed that the basis of morality must be some feature
of the world like the Idea of the Good for Plato, or nature for
Aristotle, so that the basis of morality itself gave some clue
about what one must do in order to be moral. But when you
make feelings the basis of morality, I find no clue as to what
morality should be.

*Humean:* Quite so! I have really set myself a very narrow task.
I have only tried to show what the basis of any morality is. I
have not taken on the moralist's task of recommending one
morality over all others. The morality which someone chooses,
if he does choose, is the one which he believes will enable him
to shape the world which he most desires. While I do have
definite views about the kind of world that someone ought to
desire, my ultimate defense of those views can be no different
from the defense which anyone can offer for his own moral
views; that is, I prefer mine. Either others share my preferences
or we live in different moral worlds. Moral agreement is not
to be expected between us; and the only constructive thing each
of us can do is to try to change the other's feelings.

### SUGGESTIONS FOR FURTHER READING

The most subtle, and therefore the most forceful, contemporary
statement of a Platonic kind of moral philosophy is *Principia
Ethica* by G. E. Moore (Cambridge). Moore's discussion of the
naturalistic fallacy is in Ch. 1, Part B. Hume's line of argument

is carried on in *Utilitarianism* by John Stuart Mill and in *Human Society in Ethics and Politics* by Bertrand Russell (Simon and Schuster, New York, 1955).

*Ethics* by Patrick Nowell-Smith (Penguin) is a good examination of the logic of moral arguments, a subject on which modern moral philosophers place particular emphasis. *The Language of Morals* by R. M. Hare (Oxford University Press, New York, 1952) is also recommended.

## SEVEN

Certain notions that have figured in philosophers' answers to the question, "What is a good state?" are examined in this chapter. The following items are recommended for joint reading: For the Idea of the Good, *Republic* by Plato; for nature and natural law, "De Legibus" in *Laws* and *Republic* by Cicero (Harvard, Loeb Classical Library), *Political Ideas of St. Thomas Aquinas,* edited by D. Bigongiari (Hafner), and "Nature" in *Nature and Utility of Religion* by John Stuart Mill (Liberal Arts); for philosophy of history, "Idea of a Universal History from a Cosmopolitan Point of View" by Immanuel Kant in *Theories of History* edited by P. Gardiner (Free Press, Chicago, Ill., 1959); for social contract, *The Social Contract* by J. J. Rousseau and *The Fundamental Principles of the Metaphysic of Morals* by Immanuel Kant.

# Philosophy and Politics

Traditionally, political philosophers have considered the question, "What is a good state?" I shall examine four different answers to this question which may be summarized as statements of the principle to be observed in order to bring the ideal state into existence: The ideal state must be founded and governed in the light of the Idea of the Good; the ideal state must foster in its citizens a morality consonant with the dictates of nature; the ideal state must enable its citizens to live in accordance with the purpose of history; and the ideal state must be based on a social contract.

## The State and Plato's Idea of the Good

In the *Republic* Plato offers a long answer to the question, "What is a good state?" His ultimate point is that the ideal state is one that is founded and governed in the light of the Idea of the

Good. The steps in the answer may be summarized in this way: The *Republic* begins as a discussion of the question, "What is justice?" This question may be taken in two ways. It may be the question, "What is a just man?" or it may be the question, "In what sort of state is justice obtainable?" Plato chooses to discuss the latter question as a means to answering the former, because he regards a state as a man writ large. He gives an account of his ideal state by describing the classes which it will contain and considering how harmony is to be achieved among them. From top to bottom, his classes are the rulers, the army, and the rest. The rest are variously farmers, herdsmen, artisans, and tradesmen. A distinctive feature of Plato's ideal state is that all children are the common property of the state. They are separated from their parents at birth and reared at state expense in the interest of the state. By observing a child's response to the education which the state prescribes, the rulers will be able to assess each child's powers and decide whether he is to be one of the ruled for the rest of his life or whether he is a likely candidate for the ruler class, training for which includes membership in the army. The principle, then, which governs class membership in Plato's state is that everyone is finally placed in the class for which he is fitted; and by everyone's being where he belongs, the harmonious relation of the classes is assured. The rulers rule; the ruled obey; and there is no friction.

At this point we must ask, "What fits a person to rule?" Plato's answer is that those citizens who pass into the ruling class are entitled to do so because they are able to apprehend the Idea of the Good. This ability fits them to rule because, given their knowledge, it is then certain that the state will always be ordered in accordance with the Idea of the Good. One might suppose that if such a state with such knowledgeable rulers were established, it would last forever. But at this point Plato's allegiance to the Greek view of history overwhelms his political metaphysics. For the Greeks, the movement of history was cyclic. The more things change, the sooner history will return to its starting point, only to begin repeating itself once more. Plato thought that even his ideal state would be caught in the cycle of history, and thus fall away from its perfection. Clearly there seems to be a contradiction in the belief that government in accordance with the Idea of the Good could succumb to the force of history. That Plato allows it must be attributed to some irresolution in his thought; but that he does allow it must certainly be counted among the objections to his description of the good state.

The principal objections to Plato's politics derive from the difficulties in knowing the Idea of the Good. I have already examined these difficulties at some length in Chapter 3, so I shall not repeat myself, but merely draw their consequences here. Given the enormous difficulties in getting to know the Idea of the Good, how can we be sure that any ruler will ever get to know it? From the nature of the Idea of the Good, it appears that knowing it is a very personal process. Therefore, even if one of the rulers did get to know the Idea, how could he be sure that any other ruler knows it? Given the contention that only a few people will ever be suited for the task of trying to know the Idea of the Good, it follows that no member of any other class can ever be sure that their rulers are fit to rule. What is more, it follows that only the rulers can be sure that their policies will enable the state to conform to the Idea of the Good. The only evidence available to other classes would be the negative evidence of the collapse of the state; but by then nothing could be done to save it. These difficulties in employing the Idea of the Good in politics seem to make it of doubtful use in founding the ideal state.

But we may still ask, "Has Plato at least described the constitution of the ideal state in the *Republic,* no matter how difficult it might be to achieve it?" By Plato's own standards, the answer to this question must be "No." The speakers in the *Republic* who frame the ideal state are Socrates, Glaucon, and Polemarchus. Now neither Glaucon nor Polemarchus claims to have any knowledge of the Idea of the Good. What is more, Socrates claims that it is beyond his powers to give any direct account of it. But if this is so, we cannot suppose that they have sketched the outlines of the ideal state. For they are represented as speaking without that knowledge which according to Plato is essential to the identification of the ideal state.

## APPEALS TO NATURE AND TO NATURAL LAW

I now want to consider the kind of answer to the question, "What is a good state?" which in some way invokes the criterion that the good is that which is in accord with nature or natural law. Such appeals are the descendants of Aristotle's doctrine that everything has its own peculiar tendency which it seeks to follow. Or sometimes, everything is said to have its own unique purpose or end which it seeks to fulfill. A knowledge of something's tendency or purpose or end is said to be a knowledge of its nature; and any statement of this knowledge is a natural law.

What answer follows from this doctrine, when the question, "What is a good state?" is asked? Since a state is an association of men, it may be qualified in the following way: Negatively considered, the state must not be an association which hinders a man in the fulfillment of his nature; and, positively considered, the state should be an association which enables a man to fulfill his nature. Thus the excellence of the constitution and laws of any state may be measured against the extent to which the state enables its citizens to fulfill their nature. The question for us then is, "How is this test to be applied to any given state?"

To make the test easier to apply, we must make it more definite. Instead of trying to deal with the unwieldly concept, "man's nature," let us consider some aspect of man's nature, for example, the propensity for sexual union. I choose it because this is a subject which is often discussed in the light of fulfilling nature, or conducting oneself in accordance with natural law, in the hope of characterizing the most moral condition under which sexual union in marriage should take place. It is said that the end of sexual union is the generation of children; that it is immoral to prevent the accomplishment of a natural end. Therefore any sexual union in which this consequence is prevented by a contraceptive agent is a violation of natural law, and is immoral.[1]

How can it be said that *the* end of sexual union is the generation of children? The justification for such a claim is the criterion of ultimate consequence. Such a criterion would successfully counter the claim that the pleasure of the participants is equally an end in sexual union. For since the birth of a child is a consequence ulterior to the pleasure of the participants, the generation of children appears on these grounds to be the natural end of sexual union. Therefore, sexual union ought never to be accompanied by the use of contraceptive agents; and in the interest of the morality of its citizens no state can permit their use; and in so far as its government conforms in this way to the precepts of natural law, it is a good state.

But let us see how informative the criterion of ultimate consequence is as the clue to the natural. The question to be asked is, "Which consequence is to be counted as the ultimate?" It is true that a consequence of sexual union may be the birth of a child. But the birth of a child is part of the population growth of the world. Today we are told by responsible students of these matters that an unchecked increase in the world's population will finally lead to a world in which the rate of population growth will outstrip the rate of possible food production, or even the availability of living space, with consequent misery and starvation for many. Figuring that the net increase in world population was forty-seven million in 1958 and that it would be more than fifty million in 1959, the noted biologist Sir Julian Huxley has said, "If the

---

[1] This view is put in the following way in a statement issued by the Chancery Office of the Roman Catholic Archdiocese of New York City and published in full in *The New York Times,* July 24, 1958, pp. 27 and 51:

"The conjugal act, studied from the nature of man himself, confirmed by the teaching of our Judaeo-Christian heritage, is not and can never be merely an expression of physical and biological laws. It cannot be exercised exclusively for mutual gratification. Its purpose is more ennobling—the fulfillment of the primary end of marriage in the procreation of offspring. The natural law commands that the married state, as ordained by God, fulfill the function of the conservation of the human race.

"Artificial birth control frustrates that purpose. It is, therefore, unnatural, since it is contrary to the nature and dignity of man in the exercise of his faculties and subverts the sacredness of marriage."

rate of increase continues all the space available for human existence on earth will have been taken up in less than a thousand
years. . . ." [2] To this prediction of an over-crowded world we
may add these words on feeding an ever-expanding world population by the well-known historian, Professor Arnold Toynbee,
". . . the resources of this planet, even if scientifically adminis-
tered and developed and husbanded for the benefit of the whole
human family won't suffice forever to feed a population that is
increasing ad infinitum.

"Sooner or later, food production will reach its limit. If the
population is then still increasing, famine alone will execute the
role that was played in the past by famine, pestilence and war
combined." [3]

Now at what point are we to say, "Ah, there is the ultimate
consequence of sexual union." If we apply the criterion strictly,
we must stop at, say, world starvation, which is thus shown to be
the natural consequence of unqualified sexual union. But while
the consequence may be natural, must we call it moral? I take
it that on its face any morality which appeared to sanction the
starvation of the world, or some similar calamity, is patently
absurd.

What should we expect the moralist of nature to recommend,
then? Abstention from sexual union? But this would be a curious
recommendation, for sexual union is clearly natural; and to advise against it is to admit that the natural is not an unfailing
criterion of the moral. Should he recommend the use of contra-

---

[2] *The New York Times*, November 20, 1959, p. 33. The following predictions
provide further background for Sir Julian's remarks:
   "From the time of the first man and woman it took thousands of years for the
race to reach the number of one billion living people. That occurred about 1830.
It required only one century to add the second billion—around 1930. It is now
taking less than 35 years for world population to add a third billion—probably
before 1965.
   "According to the most recent estimate of the United Nations it will take only
15 years to add the fourth billion and another 10 years to add the fifth billion.
Six or seven billion people will be living on this planet at the end of this cen-
tury—in the lifetime of many of us—*if nothing is done to arrest the growth.*"
(From *The Population Bomb*, p. 20, published and distributed by the Hugh
Moore Fund, New York.) See also *On Population: Three Essays* by Thomas
Malthus, Julian Huxley, and Frederick Osborn (Mentor).

[3] *The New York Times*, November 3, 1959, p. 8.

ceptive agents, then? He might argue that, since intelligence is a particularly human characteristic, it is natural for mankind to use that intelligence to ward off disaster. Now world starvation would certainly be a disaster; and one of the most intelligent ways of averting it is by checking world population growth through the use of contraceptive agents. As such a course would be natural, it would therefore be moral. But while this argument makes a moral appeal to the natural, surely it weakens the value of such an appeal. For it makes it appear that the use of contraceptive agents is as natural as not using them. When nature speaks both ways, can an appeal to nature be morally decisive?

Notice that when it is said that to be moral a man ought to conform to natural law, there can be no denying that man is free not to do what is said to be natural. Indeed, such a denial would vitiate the moral credit in being natural. So that in moral matters there is no sense in which I can be said to be bound by nature to one course of action over another. But then "natural" in this context means no more than "whatever is possible"; and no possible human action or consequence can be counted as unnatural. Of course, to take this point of view squeezes the moral advantage out of the label "natural." Since there are many "naturals," "natural" loses the singleness that would make it a suitable moral criterion; and the foundation of morality as well as the standard for defining a good state must be sought elsewhere.

There is also a certain absurdity in moral appeals to nature and laws of nature which it will be salutary to exhibit. On the view that the unhindered course of nature is morally desirable, a man who falls ill ought to let his disease fulfill its nature. The good sense of his physician, and the skill of his pharmacist, are contraceptive to the natural course of the disease within him. How can the natural moralist call his physician, take his medicine, and circumvent nature by clinging to life?

The naturalist replies: "You have this all wrong. What we have here are two bits of nature, a man and the gang of germs which it attacking him. The proper question is, 'Which is more valuable, the man or the germs?' I say, 'The man'; and he ought to take his medicine. It's the natural thing to do."

The anti-naturalist: "Notice that you have had to skip outside of nature to justify medicine. The germs are just as natural as the man. Of course, I agree that the man is more valuable than the germs; but this point is nowhere discoverable in nature. It must be introduced into the situation by your judgment. The force of this point is immediately apparent if you only consider what we should hear if we were able to listen to the germs. My claim must be that nature is morally neutral, and that the natural is no clue to the moral."

The naturalist: "Well, I must admit that I have one last string to my bow. I am not an unmitigated naturalist. I believe that there is a god above nature, and that both nature and man are subject to him. He is revealed to us through nature; but the course of nature is not the sum total of his will for us."

The anti-naturalist: "This amendment of your position will take us farther afield than the original issue. Without prejudice, then, to your new criterion, the will of a god, I must say this much about nature and morality. A man must order the course of his life as he sees fit, taking guidance where he can find it. His safest course is to consider the consequences of his actions and act accordingly; but, while a knowledge of the natural will tell him what is possible, only experience of life can tell him what is preferable. I submit then that since the criteria of morality are not to be found in nature, there is no possibility of assessing the excellence of a state by determining whether it enables its citizens to order their lives in conformity with natural law."

## APPEALS TO HISTORY

I now want to turn to answers to the question, "What is a good state?" which take the form, "A state will be a good state in so far as it enables its citizens to live according to the purpose of history." The gist of these answers is that human history is a march toward some predetermined goal, and that the good state is one which will enable its citizens to participate in the march. In a bad state, the constitution is opposed to the course of history; and thus its citizens are "swimming against the current"

with all the consequent agony to themselves and to the rest of
the human race which must remain near them. There are several
questions which suggest themselves here. What is meant by "history"? Can history march, flow, proceed, progress, etc.? Can history have a goal? Can we know what the goal of history is?
When we find out the answers to these questions, we shall be in
a position to judge whether or not an appeal may be made to history to justify a particular kind of state.

In this context "history" means each person's living his life,
doing his job, and taking his ease, so that an observer looking
down on a given society, or even the whole of the human race,
can see a pattern emerging from the way in which every person's
deeds interact with those of everyone else. To our favored observer this ever-changing pattern sometimes seems to have a life
of its own, so that it can be thought about independently of the
individuals from whose lives it has been abstracted. What is
more, this pattern is sometimes thought of as imposing demands
on individual human beings, demands to which they must conform; so that history, the pattern, makes the individual rather
than their making history.

This is such a remarkable and, as we now know, world-shak-
ing view to take of human beings and their lives that some account of its origin must be given. The kind of view which I have
been describing is one of the things which is called philosophy
of history,[4] and the observer who takes this kind of view is called
a philosopher of history. Philosophy of history became an independent subject, worthy of study in its own right, in the late
eighteenth century. But before this time it had a long life em-
bedded in the Jewish and Christian religions. The foundation of
Judaism is the Eternal's contract with Abraham to be his god
and the god of his descendants and to provide them a home in
"the land of Canaan." One of the most enthralling story threads
in the Old Testament is the account of God's fulfilling his prom-

---

[4] The other two generally recognized meanings of the "philosophy of history"
are (1) a more "scientific" variety of the kind of philosophy of history described
above, in which predictions of the future are regarded only as probable and not
predetermined, and (2) a study of the principles of historiography (What kinds
of evidence are available for the historian's statements, etc.).

ise to the Jews. That story has several features important to the philosophy of history. By reading it, one learns to think in great sweeps of time. One learns to think of people who have importance, and consequently a history, as a group. One learns to think of a group of people bound by a destiny that is greater than the group itself. Without membership in the group the individual is as nothing; but by his membership the character of his individual fate is determined by the fate of the group.

As might be expected from its origins in Judaism, Christianity also has a philosophy of history. God makes a promise to the Christian group, too; but instead of promising to locate them in an earthly land of Canaan, God offers to unite Christians with him in heaven. Because of its difference from Judaism, in that in Christianity one can only join the Christian group by one's own choice whereas in Judaism the fact of birth directs one firmly toward membership in the group, Christianity has certain special features in its philosophy of history. One must, of course, join the favored group for oneself; and, in theory at least, everyone is given a chance to join. This, I believe, is Christianity's principal contribution to philosophy of history's general stock of ideas. But woe unto those who do not become Christians, for God has a punishment in store for them just as surely as he has a reward ready for his favored group. The lesson for philosophy of history here is that there is a knowable fate in store for each of us. No one can expect to escape; and the pleasantness of our ends depends on whether we are in harmony with the powers that govern the world.

How did the philosophy of history come to be a study in its own right, independent of religious revelation? The break was made possible by the growth of religious radicalism after the Reformation. Among intellectuals there was a widespread interest in achieving a reasonable knowledge of God by inferring his nature from the order which they found in the world. But in the course of their studies, philosophers lost sight of the god of Judaism and Christianity; and nature itself (in Kant), the world spirit (in Hegel), and dialectical materialism as personified in the class struggle (in Marx) took on the tasks that in a religion are assigned to a god. Thus rational religion slides into philosophy of history; but the divine paternity of these historical forces must not be forgotten.

It is time to look at one of these philosophies of history. The one which I have chosen to discuss is Kant's, which he describes in his essay, "The Idea of a Universal History on a Cosmopolitical Plan." Kant begins by noticing that a certain kind of pattern is discoverable in human affairs. For instance, marriages may be regarded from the point of view of particular unions or one may take a more elevated view of the human scene and regard marriage as a social statistic, paying attention, he says, to the regularity of the number of marriages which occur in a given country in each year, and, we may add, paying attention in addition to the relation of the number of marriages to other social statistics. As the statistics of marriage exemplify, there is then a pattern of human affairs greater than any individual; and our question is, "How is this pattern to be discovered?" Kant's answer to this question is a peculiar one. We might say that there is a pattern in human affairs; and it is to be found in the statistical generalizations about social behavior which we have just considered. But this answer will not do for Kant, because, not only must there be a pattern in human affairs, but this now shifting pattern must have some final form to which it tends, and, what is more, to which it tends inexorably. Notice that there might be some final form to which the pattern of human affairs does tend; but if we described that form simply on the basis of our knowledge of human affairs now and in the past, our description would only be probable, and matters could turn out differently. But this chancy view is just what Kant does not want. He wants philosophy of history to describe *the* end of human affairs.

What Kant offers as his philosophy of history is a set of principles in accordance with which human affairs are to be viewed. Briefly stated, his principles are that there is above us all a force called nature; that nature has imposed on everything an end toward which it tends (notice the paralleling of Aristotle here); that the end of man is the perfection of the human species (he argues that it is obvious from the fact that men are individually

weak that nature does not seek the perfection of individuals);
that the perfection of the human species will be achieved only in
a world state; that, hence, the organization of the human species
in a world-wide state is the goal toward which the unfolding pattern of human affairs tends.

The most important question to be asked about Kant's philosophy of history is, "How can we be sure that there is a force
which he calls nature, which operates in human affairs?" Kant's
evidence seems to be that, since human beings have been *made*
too weak to live independently, it is obvious that they have been
*made* to live interdependently in larger and larger complexes
of interdependence. However, by regarding human beings as
having been *made* by an intelligent creator, we immediately assume the point which an inspection of human beings and their
affairs is supposed to prove. But even though the existence of
Kant's presiding nature is doubtful, it still might be true that
human beings who are by nature too weak to live independently
must of necessity learn to live interdependently. The point at issue
now is just this jump from the way Kant sees people to be and
the way they *must* live to compensate for it. Kant may be right
in his view that it would be best for people to live in a world
state; but it is one thing to have a belief about what would be
good for the human race and another thing to believe that the
good must come about. By confusing these two kinds of belief,
Kant comes to the conclusion that the organization of the human
species in a world-wide state cannot fail to come about; but it
is difficult to know how he could argue for this claim. If the
claim is matter-of-fact, then what he sees to be the good may
or may not come about; and thus he should not argue that it
must. On the other hand, if his claim is matter-of-logic, it must
necessarily be true; but then it would be not about the world but
only about his conception of the way the world should be. So his
claim cannot be matter-of-logic, for philosophy of history must
be about world events, if it is about anything; and we are driven
back to regarding his claim as matter-of-fact. Therefore, I do
not see how Kant could argue that human affairs *must* be taking

a particular direction, no matter how attractive Kant might find
that direction himself.

There is yet another difficulty in Kant's philosophy of history.
It is the way he slips from the activities of individual persons to
the pattern of human affairs, so that the pattern becomes a super-
individual, incorporating all human beings, and with tendencies
and goals of its own. If we can divest ourselves of this notion, we
can see that there is no room for frightening questions about *the*
end to which human affairs are tending. There may be an end;
but it is the end which human beings themselves are responsible
for, in varying degrees, depending on their powers and oppor-
tunities. The end of human affairs which Kant perceives, the
harmonious union of the human species in a world state, may
be admirable in the extreme; but there can be no guarantee that
this is *the* end of human affairs.

Certain of the verbs which earlier I coupled with history can
now be seen to be figures of speech. To talk of "the march of
history" is to objectify the pattern of human affairs in the form
of a regiment, and then to smuggle in inferences favorable to
the philosophy of history. Just as a regiment marches to some
destination, so history advances on its goal. Talk of history's pro-
ceeding or progressing also shares the strength of the military
allusion just noticed. "The flow of history" objectifies history as
a river; and just as rivers finally meet the sea, so history too can
have a goal. To see through these, and other, objectifications of
history is to see part of the answer to the question, "Can history
have a goal?" The answer is "Yes" only if you choose to look
at history as if it had a goal. For the rest, one must remember
the religious origins of the philosophy of history.

Because philosophy of history leaves us uncertain about what it
is we know or indeed whether we know anything at all, when
we suppose that we know the goal of history, I submit that
claims that a state should enable its citizens to live according to
the purpose of history are poor answers to the question, "What
is a good state?" It is true that Kant, for example, as a philosopher
of history, may be said to advocate a world state, and other philosophers of history give other pieces of political advice; but on

examining their work, it will be found that their philosophies of history afford little reason for following their political advice. Whether the advice itself is of value must be determined on other grounds.

## SOCIAL CONTRACT

I want now to consider the claim that a good state is one that is based on a social contract. I shall discuss this claim as it is made by Rousseau, noticing also Kant's variations on Rousseau's doctrines. "Social contract" is a concept which has had a long history in political philosophy. It is discussed briefly in the early part of Plato's *Republic,* for example; and in the last three hundred years it has been an increasingly important idea in political thought.

The idea of a social contract was invented by philosophers who were interested in providing a rational basis for human association in a state. How are we to understand "rational basis" here? Force, for instance, might provide a basis for association, but would it be a rational basis? No, because the use of force is antithetical to association. When the machine guns are jammed, the people made to associate by force of arms will break away. A rational basis for association, then, must be one that gives the association the best chance of lasting, for such a basis is the only one that is consistent with the notion of association. How does the idea of a social contract provide a rational basis for association?

In the first place, it must be admitted that no political association has a chance of being formed unless the people who are to enter into it believe that association is more valuable than independence; and the association will last only so long as they continue to believe it. Now under what conditions could association be more valuable than independence? The consideration which is regularly introduced at this point is that most men are naturally ill-fitted to live alone. The abilities of any one man are never so great that co-operating with others will not be to his advantage; and the hardness of life regularly dictates such co-

operation. What is more, if there is no social life, there is but a
dim prospect of keeping whatever one has wrested from nature.
In Hobbes's famous phrase, life without society is "nasty, brutish
and short." The advantages of co-operation appear to be clear.
The question is, what scheme of co-operation would best maintain the association?

Here I wish to introduce Rousseau's answer. The basic article
in the social contract must be that no one is to receive any more
from the association than anyone else. It follows that in any
distribution of the goods of the association, all members are entitled to equal amounts. In return for this promise, everyone who
joins the association has a vote in determining the kind of goods
that are to be made available. Only on these conditions can association appear more advantageous than independence. But how
can an association based on these conditions be made to work?

The leading principle of Rousseau's scheme of political association is that policy decisions may be made only in meetings at
which all members of the association are present and able to vote.
In return for the right to vote, all members of the association
agree to abide by the decision of the majority, so that as soon as
the majority decision is known, it becomes, in Rousseau's words,
"the will of all." Rousseau is adamant on the point that each
member of the association must vote only as he himself determines; that is, he must never regard himself as a member of a
party within the state, nor must he ever delegate the power of
casting his vote to a representative. He must vote only after he
has asked of the policy in question, "Will it be for the good of
all?" "Good of all" must mean here that everyone may gain
the same kind and the same amount of advantage from this
policy; and in addition, that the members of the association will
not enjoy a given advantage at the expense of some greater advantage.

Now this political scheme of Rousseau's suggests a fascinating
question which he does not answer, and which I am not sure
that he should be expected to answer. It is, "What policies would
be for the good of all?" All we may gather from Rousseau is that
it is no good saying that a society ought to follow those policies

which will be for the good of all; for it can follow no others and last. For the rest, we may suppose that time and place will suggest certain policies to the members of the association. What these policies might be, it is pointless to describe or discuss beforehand. All that can be done is to give a rule for choosing those policies which can be followed without destroying the association, i.e. those which benefit all members of the association equally. This is all Rousseau ever hoped to do.

What points are sometimes raised against Rousseau's scheme of political arrangements? Let it be said at the outset that it is not fair to charge Rousseau with reducing individual liberty in order to make men into social beings. Political association is impossible without surrendering some individual liberty. Rousseau is writing only for those people who already believe association to be a good thing. To disagree is to start a quite different topic from the one which Rousseau treats.

It is sometimes said, as though it were a point against Rousseau, that it would be impossible to achieve the political scheme which he describes. For instance, Rousseau thought that the ideal state should not have more than 10,000 members, and that the state of the world and the mode of the citizens' lives should be such that a single annual meeting would be sufficient to settle the policy questions of the association. But clearly we today must think in terms of states very much larger than Rousseau's ideal, if not indeed a world state; and what is more, even in the best of the present states a representative government is the regular arrangement. I should be the first to admit that the political arrangements which Rousseau describes are difficult to achieve; but he is still to be commended for having described them. For by giving us an account of what a true association would be, he has given us a standard by which to judge how far we are from achieving it.

There are, however, two difficulties in Rousseau's social contract which must be noticed. The first comes to light when one asks how the political rights of children are to be provided for. Since ideally each person can contract only for himself, no parent can contract for his children. But if children are not part of the association, they are a possible source of disruption. This puzzle is not peculiar to Rousseau. It crops up in any society of which children are a part. The solution would seem to be that children must be made to feel social obligation as quickly as possible so that a sense of responsibility is implanted in them even before they become aware of the social rights they may enjoy. But it must be admitted that talk of social obligations without awareness of corresponding rights is nonsense to Rousseau; and only serves to point up the difficulty of introducing children into an association based on social contract.

The other difficulty that I wish to notice is not so much a difficulty as it is a distressing feature of Rousseau's social contract; at least many people find it distressing. How is a member of the association who refuses to abide by the majority will to be dealt with? He must be compelled to be free. Rousseau's point is that, having joined the association and having had a vote in the determination of the majority will, a member can only be consistent by abiding by the majority decision. Each member of the association is entitled to expect consistency from every other member; and any member who fails to be consistent breaks his tie with the association. Those who remain in the association must either compel the offending member to be consistent or cast him from their midst, lest his continued presence cause the association to founder. Rousseau regards the kind of consistency described here as rational freedom. Hence, compelling someone to be consistent with his original promise to abide by the majority will would be, for Rousseau, compelling someone to be free. Defenders of unqualified individualism may find this a hard view to accept; but it must be remembered that Rousseau is writing about someone who has turned against an association which he freely joined and not about someone who is being crushed by a state which he had no part in originating.

Now this sounds all very well, but Rousseau's position only serves to raise the question, "In what sense can someone be said to join a state?" We know all about taking out citizenship papers, of course; but the comparative rarity of immigration only serves to point up the fact that by far the greater number of people in the world are simply born into the state in which they live and die. How this situation is to be rationalized, if it is to be rationalized at all, is not explained by Rousseau. He does not show us how to make sense of the notion that someone joins the state into which he is born; and both the present territorial organization of the world and the pressures of world population make it doubtful that very many people can find a fresh part of the world in which to form a new state on the lines Rousseau recommends.

It might be worth our while then to turn to Kant's efforts to show how Rousseau's kind of state could be brought into existence. Kant, who, as we have seen, might be called after his own style a cosmopolitical thinker, believed that a world-wide state embracing the human race was both necessary and inevitable for the good of mankind. But bringing such a state into existence requires the simplest possible methods of joining the state and knowing its laws. Kant solved these difficulties in the following way. The state needs to have only one law, the Categorical Imperative: Act only on a maxim which you can will to be a universal law. Or to put it more plainly, perhaps: Always do what you would have everyone else do when in your position. As for joining Kant's state, one becomes a citizen simply by imposing this law on oneself. In effect, Kant has accepted the criterion which is to guide the members of Rousseau's social contract when they are annually assembled as a legislature; but he has gone Rousseau one better. His legislature is always in session. What is more, he has made clear the necessity of emphasizing the principles of the social contract in private life as well; indeed, under Kant's law, morals and politics are indistinguishable.

My reason for doing only what I would have anyone in my position do is that only by acting in this way can I hope to maintain society. By acting otherwise, falsely promising to repay a loan, for example, I demand special privilege for myself. If I lie, however, I cannot consistently deny everyone else the right to lie. But if lying were to become the universal rule, there could be no trust, and social life would be impossible. If I value society, then I can never promise falsely to repay a loan, or for that matter, act in any other way that I would forbid to the rest of mankind on the grounds of its harmfulness to society. This is the only course consistent with my long-term desire to maintain society; and no reasonable man could act otherwise.

But it must be admitted that Kant's improvements on Rousseau are not without their own difficulties; and the first is, I fear, an insuperable one. What are we to do with someone who says, "I am going to lie whenever lying will get me out of a tight spot; and I really don't care if everyone else does the same thing." We may say to him, "You are wrecking society, you know," and he may very well reply, "I don't mind that either." States do seem to exist to drag along people who have no intention of going peaceably; and as long as there are such people it seems that we must have states. What we should like Kant to tell us is how to deal with the anti-social. Could they be reformed? Must they be locked up for our own good, if not theirs? But like the enlightened man of the eighteenth century that he was, Kant believed that no rational person could be anti-social. I am afraid that taking this line commits one to assuming anti-social people out of existence, a course which we may see to be unreasonable if not actually self-destructive.

In the second place, I think we must complain that what Kant gives us is really not a state at all. By itself the observance of the Categorical Imperative is insufficient machinery for carrying out those large projects that are beyond the powers of one or a few individuals and for the accomplishment of which states exist. Both Kant and Rousseau are to be respected for trying to make governmental policy everybody's business. But such efforts appear to be in various ways self-defeating. For there does seem to be a practical point beyond which government that is everybody's business becomes nobody's business. Nonetheless the limitations which the practical imposes upon us may gain our forbearance more easily, once we have explored the ideal schemes of Rousseau and Kant.

The position of the twentieth-century reader of political philosophy deserves a special word. The question that he is likely to ask is not, "What is a good state?" but "Why should I be a citizen at all?" This question would have been unthinkable to the ancient Greeks. Membership in a city-state was an integral part of their conception of a person. As Aristotle puts it, the man who can live alone must be either a beast or a god. But the apolitical origin of Christianity has given us a different point of view. It is possible to think of loyalty to God or loyalty to conscience as taking precedence over loyalty to the state. What is more, the lack of a modern ceremony of acceptance into citizenship, except for immigrants, is a further sign that the state is a flimsy kind of association. As citizenship becomes a negligible responsibility, the connection between the state and the government grows more tenuous; and the officers of government tend to form an association within the larger association. Since the state is no longer an end in itself, its form and policies may be judged by external standards derived from the religion and morals of its citizens. Thus, the political philosopher who lives in Christian times, particularly post-Reformation times, and who says a good word for the state must be on the defensive in a way that his ancient Greek predecessors never had to be.

If the modern political philosopher has any tasks imposed on him by the times, one of them must surely be that of reconciling the claims of individualism with what is for most of us the undeniable necessity of having to live in some kind of political association. The political philosopher may of course try to remove the conflict by discovering some hitherto unnoticed fact about the world in whose light the conflict sinks into insignificance. There is, however, a less dramatic but in the long run a possibly more rewarding course for the political philosopher. He may attempt not to dissolve the conflict we feel between individualism and association but to help us understand it by giving us an analysis of both the claims of individualism and the forms and purposes of association. When we know where we are, we shall then be able to tell which way we must go.

SUGGESTIONS FOR FURTHER READING

*The Vocabulary of Politics* by T. D. Weldon (Penguin) is the best general book on philosophy and politics. Two classic works on individualism and political association are the essay "Civil Disobedience" by Henry David Thoreau and *On Liberty* by John Stuart Mill. A more recent book on the same theme is *Authority and the Individual* by Bertrand Russell (Beacon).

There are many philosophies of history. Two of the earliest and for that reason most influential are the Hegelian and the Marxist. For the former, see *Lectures on the Philosophy of History* by G. W. F. Hegel (Dover). For Marxism see *The Communist Manifesto* and the essay "Socialism: Utopian and Scientific" by Friedrich Engels. Both are reprinted in *Basic Writings on Politics and Philosophy* by Karl Marx and Friedrich Engels, edited by L. S. Feuer (Doubleday Anchor). One of the best criticisms of philosophy of history as a discipline is *The Poverty of Historicism* by Karl Popper (Beacon Press, Boston, 1957). Three good books about philosophies of history are *The Idea of History* by R. G. Collingwood (Oxford Galaxy), *Philosophy of History: An Introduction* by W. H. Walsh (Harper Torchbooks) and *Meaning in History, The Theological Implications of the Philosophy of History* by Karl Löwith (University of Chicago Phoenix).

# Index